LEMON PEELED
THE MOMENT BEFORE

New & Selected Poems 1967—2008

Roger Mitchell

T0162020

AUSABLE PRESS
2008

Cover art: "Weather. Mt. Provencher" by Linda Fisher, 2005
Oil on panel. 19.75" x 19.75"

Author photo: www.wblstudio.com
Design and composition by Ausable Press
The type is Garamond.
Cover design by Rebecca Soderholm

Published by
AUSABLE PRESS
1026 HURRICANE ROAD
KEENE, NY 12942
www.ausablepress.org

Distributed to the trade by
CONSORTIUM BOOK SALES & DISTRIBUTION
34 THIRTEENTH AVENUE NE, SUITE 101
MINNEAPOLIS, MN 55413-1007
(612) 746-2600
FAX: (612) 746-2606
Orders: (800) 283-3572

Library of Congress Cataloging-in-Publication Data

Mitchell, Roger, 1935—
Lemon peeled the moment before: new and selected poems,
1967-2008 / Roger Mitchell. —1st ed.
p.cm.
ISBN 978-1-931337-41-0 (pbk. : alk. paper)
I. Title
PS3563.I82L38 2008
811'.54—dc22
2008032808

for Dorian

CONTENTS

from *Adirondack*

from *The Word For Everything*

from *Braid*

from *Savage Baggage*

from *The One Good Bite in the Saw Grass Plant*

from *Delicate Bait*

from *Half/Mask*

New Poems

Letters From Siberia and Other Poems (1971)

NATTY BUMPPO

I
Natty Bumppo wades through the sunken prairie
under the house.
He talks to the stuffed dog of his mind,
close at his heels,
about the philosophical implications
of billboards.
The dog offers its worn hairless ear
to scratch,
as Natty, in clod-soft speech
carries the syntax
of his endless sentence
on the virtues of silence and cunning
deeper into the earth.
Natty Bumppo wades through flames,
descending, looking for water.
All around him, the prairie is on fire.
The flames snap like a purse above his head.

II
I, too, am the last of my race,
passing on, if anything,
the urge to be last, again.

III
Natty Bumppo knocks on the door at midnight
with an armload of brooms.
His pin-stripe suit has a coonskin collar

and the stripes light up in the dark.
"The misses' musket," Natty winks
and shoots the soot off the windowsill.

Natty does the frug on my front porch.
He hums and claps in the star-pinched dark
for thirty seconds, stops
in mid bump,
and sings The Star-Spangled Banner.

IV
Natty enters my bedroom
dressed in red.
He chuckles to the axes
in back of my mind—
come to the prairie, you bastards.

Natty stands in a blur of fire.
The tips of his words burn white
when he speaks of that first felled tree,
implosion of sunlight,
of the bloodless stump
rotting, in a tuft of weeds
in the crotch of a dark bay.

I lie on a Kansas of sheet
and listen to Natty urging me west
where the axe can't bite.
His locked jaw whispers, come.

He fires his empty musket over my head.
Flame spurts from the iron barrel.
The wings of the curtains flutter down.

The old boy scout heads west alone,
full of a celibate fire.
Kill, he roars, firing into the clouds,
kill,
and the sun falls down.

THE SIX O'CLOCK NEWS

for Sylvia Plath

I see the carcass of another nun,
burnt stiff. It topples like a doll, slowly,
as though the flames were there to ease it down.
Her head, made of finer stuff than Christmas
ornaments, bursts in a rainbow of outrage.
Another perfect mind rots in the street
like a discarded flower. The smell of it
reaches me all the way from Saigon.
I'll never wear such a flower, or know
the blossoming of a thought so fierce
that it could push blood back where it came from,
packing it tight, till the swollen sack bursts.
But I know something of that desire,
to make the world a buttonhole affair
and toss it, light as breath, on the mind's pyre.
So, every night at six o'clock I watch
while the pure idea puts forth its petals.
In a low crackle of ancient static,
I listen to speeches, see villages bombed,
watch reputations born, all in time
to this constant slosh of blood against the heart.
The soft plastic click, as I turn it off,
is as friendly as a heart beat can be.

WHAT IT IS

I have no clear idea what it is,
that being part of it, but sometimes
it comes into the room as if looking,
a little desperate, but indifferent,
anxious, but not ever for you and not
of course staying any longer
than to say, "I've lost someone,"
then leaving, through a watery silhouette,
a hole in the room's natural light,
as though, by going, it had torn itself
off the skin of the eyeball, opening
a way into further light, revealing,
like the cleaned corner of an old painting,
this room, for the first time, as it is.

NOVICE: ABROAD

All men are brothers, the handbook says.
My tongue swells like a park-cleaner's bag
after an autumn holiday,
rolls heavily with the refuse of speech,
hobbling it to a staggered, stoop-sided shuffle.
If a scrap escapes, it is lanced back by the odd look.
Conspicuousness fits like an accusation.
I walk through a moveable nimbus of stares,
an aluminum mold, a shining habit.
Piles of swept dirt greet me at the curb.

CHILDREN AT AUSCHWITZ
(OSWIEÇIM, POLAND)

They come here by busloads in the early fall.
The plain brick buildings and the tree-lined streets,
the neighborly curtness of "Keep Off the Grass,"
do not deceive them. This is the class trip.

This is the last cold step out of childhood
into the tepid air of right and wrong,
where for a moment in curiosity
the truth gapes. Anything is possible.

While the rest of us drag half-willing feet
from room to room, trying strange feelings on
in this strange store, looking for one that neither
hides nor exposes what we think we feel,

they plunge noisily through the corridors
searching the photographs along the walls
for their own names, or sit on the steps out front
squeezing their lunches out of paper bags.

The uncomplicated act of chewing, here,
is worth a warehouse of human hair heaped
artfully in show cases or stacked in bales.
Though it's more than bread they swallow here,

at least they haven't learned self-loathing yet.
I say this, though one of them rabbit-punches
his shadow into the wall, and kicks it,
laughing, in the nuts, to show them how it was.

THOUGHTS ON A BIRTH

I
Fresh from a bath
wrapped in a towel
stepping across the air
in 1960
a light scissoring of ankles
a fluttering
over the bare wooden floor
suspended
never still.
The memory bites into me,
a long crisp scissorstroke.

II
Then, on the same tight sheet,
the long night
of listening
for the other's breath,
the stillness
sneaking into sleep
breath
by calculated breath,
two paper cut-outs
pasted on the same page,
a mattress ad.

III
Now this,
on the night train
moving south from Warsaw,
drumming its fingertips of light
on the frozen fields.
You concentrate like the ground,
wrinkled, on a remote tapping,
an impatience.
I sit across from you
and concentrate back.
We think the same thought
at last
like a pair of scissors.
We emerge from the folds of a long traverse
with a snap.

LETTER TO MILWAUKEE

As I lay last night under the knife
of your hot breath, that blade now rusted,
garbage burning in the outer suburbs,
as I lay there drawing breath and comparisons
under the weak ether of the window slit,
and the carbon depositing under my tongue,
and me being new to Milwaukee and all,
I thought of writing you.

Better than you, I like the idea of you
as something I may have seen in an old dream
briefly before forgetting, and coming across you
in both of our hag-ridden middle years,
which is a loaded conception
but one that will do to give us an air
of respectability in our first throat-clearing
moments together before whatever ensues.

You have a mind of dirt, the wisdom
to lie there and be walked on, to be prodded,
to be pushed anywhere except out of sight.
The black tree reaches up out of you
like a hand slipping out of sight
from the middle of a bare block under the Juneau Towers,
the glint of old sidewalks just under the stubble
and bottom steps crumbled like saved cake.

The unfinished ramp stops
at the boarded fourth-story windows
of an abandoned factory,
a frozen ejection of cement.
Dotted lines dump into the lake
beyond fresh excavations,
forums of threaded columns
rising from buried riverbanks.
Slums in the arms of interchanges,
stone octopuses wrestle the sky.

The young executives in their sideburns
sweep the sidewalks in smiling rows.
They wear each other's clothes
by way of compliment, exchange toupees
at noon under the boom of the burgherly clock.
A precarious satisfaction trickles
from their mouths, no greater than my own.

And on the south side, they say,
some have never seen the lake.
Whole educational systems have been devised
and cafeteria programs. Secretaries of awareness
in pointed sweaters
continuously patrol the boundaries
of their concrete smile, whispering,
Forget, the lake is beside you.
The disbelievers hug themselves with powerful arms
in the back rows
and dream of wrenches and good bosoms.

All over the city, the congregation of the buses
shifts, again. The intoning of advertisements
goes on silently around us,
easing the strangling of the shopping bags.
A man gets on and sits in front of me
wearing a wad of chewing gum in the middle
of his back. I think of saving him
for a moment, but he saves himself
by getting up and leaving, by walking through you
with chewing gum stuck to the middle of his back.
What have you done with him?
Whose mark was he wearing?

But like this letter, you are thinking of other things.
You want to go bowling or to your sister Rita's.
That is the nice thing about poets. You can go
to your sister Rita's and they will wait outside.
They will fetch beer if you run out
and stand in the dark counting telephone poles
until you are ready to go.
And all that time the conversation continues,
and when you pick it up four hours later
we are in the middle of the same word.

The empty stapler, the unsharpened pencil,
the dry rubberstamp of a dead executive,
instructions for the care of lenses,
the closed pipe-case, recipes for soap,
unanswered letters from Puerto Rico,
back issues still in plain brown wrappers,

bookmarks stuck into slanted texts
like flags in the sides of whales
hunted by other men in another time.

Today, I walked past the Hong Fat Co.
To have walked past the Hong Fat Co.
alone, the sun shining, and snow drifted
into the doorways of the bars across the street,
speaks for itself. Later, I walked up the hill
past the brewery where the old brick mansions
lie boarded and painted,
houses full of gothic cement,
mausoleums for the barons who built them,
each with an owner cemented into bed.

But this is no time to speak of mausoleums.
A small worm has entered your skin
through the inhaling of its pores
and swum its way to your heart
where it fills your blood like an ocean
with infinite black sperm.
The gardens of your ocean luxuriate.
The underwater movement of slow bodies,
the underwater speech, the beat of your own heart
comes back, floating on slow sperm.
You think you are poisoned and about to die,
but that is your last heart beating back.

I like it when the beautiful young Negresses
climb aboard you like a public convenience

and use you. And the gray undergraduates
sit on the stairways of glass and memorize
levels of communication. Interpersonal,
they shout through the legs of ascending professors.
Intrapersonal. And someone memorizes his name.

And some would call this fallacy pathetic.
But I do not expect you to listen to me
except in the way you might listen
to traffic at the bottom of the afternoon,
the trembling of the windowpanes,
the conversation in the next life like water
running through the walls, leaves brushing.
The bush spoke to Moses because it had to.

The eastside mansions preen against their flags.
At night the snow blows through the spotlights
on its way to the flags and lifts up the skirts
of the twinkled Christmas frontlawn everywhere
wedding of the arctic pole. At night
I walk through your orange windows and count
the leathered bookbacks, touch your blue wallpapers,
swoon for the corners of your perfect paintings.
One night I saw the eldest son in the living room.
He pushed plants into the windows, threw incense
over the piano, took off his clothes and wept.
I stood awhile and heard this weeping.
It was full of socialism and the three bears
to whom he promised more porridge in the morning
if only they would vote for him, only vote for him.

The bears, whom I could not see,
demanded more porridge, more than porridge,
porridge now. Which, when they got, promptly
put them into a deep sleep from which
it is said they will hardly ever wake.
And on the front lawns they are whistling Dixie.
And in the homes they are coaxing children
into the world, pounding their mitts of stone
and singing, "hum babe, hum that pea."

Let your houses come down.
Let them feel the bite of the crane.
Let their intimacies come into the open.
Let the walls of need stand for a moment,
their pale stains flowering the rubble.
Let the students watch on their way to class.
When you put the grass back, unroll it slowly.
Or better yet, let it come back by itself.
The silence of the prairie's vengeance,
the squeak of the ungreased grassblade,
here where it is buried, would help us.
Let there be a vacant lot in the neighborhood
with broken bricks bulldozed into a cellarhole,
a place for children to make us
and stone us in the open air.

I cannot think of you always
in the way of my grandmother's brown poems.
Nostalgia precedes my knowledge of you,
as it does of everything. Today,

in a photograph, I see my mother
for the first time, the new mother, the girl
just gone, stunned by the theft, the thief
grinning wickedly, the blob propped up
by an outspread hand, wider than memory,
furrowed with blood and the hint
of women harnessed to a dead stick
at the back of winter. And over it all,
the slack-clothed sag of the immigrant.
I see now why I am here
writing these letters to no one
in a language no one speaks.

Daily, I let poems slide past me.
I see them coming and I think of arranging
the glot of grief in my throat
and the whole exhalation machine,
but when they come, I let them go.
It must mean something to have
so many poems in one place
and to feel like leaving them where they are.
It is like the sacred cow of India
who needs no invitation, who is worshiped
by being left alone.

from READING THE NEWS

They could not believe themselves cruel,
those who had worked hard
according to the customs of that place.
But just in case,
they found leaders who flattered them,
authorized beatings by innuendo,
wars by false evidence.
At night, they pulled armchairs
up to a blue stew
and counted bodies
as they fell into it.

*

I wake at night
to a distant pounding in the wall.
It is dark, listening.
I do not realize for a long time
that it is my voice
reading the news.
There are no words to the news,
only their shadows.
Like someone beating a dead throat
with a microphone.

*

I am dreamfolded.
They take me over
a deep forest.

They give me an M-16, a compass,
a knapsack full of radioactive money.
Survive, they say,

as they shove me through the hatch.
Tell them you were captured.
We will acknowledge nothing.

If caught, kill yourself.
Something like sight blossoms over me
as I fall.

Moving (1976)

EDGES

I

For months I've walked this rocky coast,
building fires in windless cracks,
snaring birds from the air, fish
from the gray sea. One net for all,
flashing into the element.

On land I am flaky. Bits of me
break against stone. The wind looks after
my loosening hair. This falling
apart is my daily miracle.
Night is alive in another place.

II

I'm never far from edges.
Here, the land pushes into the sea.
The white eyes of the sea open
and close like stars everywhere.

I sleep on my arm, rise with it
bloodless, dragging against me, hold
it under the fire to bring it back.

Everything speaks.
Each wave is a tongue. Each stone,
a language rolled into one.
The weeds are dialects of wind
and water.

Winter is hard in these caves. The sand stings.
Summer is better, though barely.
I lie on the low rocks where land
and sea come close to each other.

III
This is the time before time,
the waves one continuous roar,
the wind a single breath,
birds the feathers of one body.
Light is a version of sight.

This is the sea without stop,
the rolling thorn that grows to itself.
This is the sky holding itself
in its cloudless arms.
This is.

IV
I lie on the hot sand for hours,
my head in the dune grass. It is dark.
Down on the beach people are dancing,
shadows staggering among flames.

The sea makes silence like a noise.
The dancers fall, exhausted, laughing.
They think they are drunk.

They smell of meat, salty and burnt.
Even now, they know what they want.
It lies on them sleeping like dew.

The fire falls, at last, like shadow.
Into itself.
The hiss whose silence is its voice
licks us into darkness.

V
The whales drift away, having seen.
The wind sucks at my ears.
The sea looks at me sideways,
wrinkling away, through its single squint.
It is time to go back.

The sky's eye rolls in its juices,
milky, looking for its own pupil,
looking for the other eye, lost,
on the far side of its head,
the eye that can see for itself.

LOOKING IN ON MY
FOUR-YEAR-OLD

How much like everything you look,
lying there, with nowhere to go,
and yet gone, full of a deep silence
like water, close to me, even
a part of me. But with the huge

impersonality of things,
flung at the bed. You might have crawled
up out of these sheets, like the sea
from which you came, to spawn your own
small motions in the elements,

mountains lifting, clouds swallowing,
moons and the long blue interludes,
lightning splitting the darkness
like an egg, the quick white spilling,
seabirds in an inland garden.

I try to arrange your limp limbs
in some semblance of what you are
awake, but you resist, even now,
fierce for the distance between us,
the self you don't know you must bear.

FROM ENGLAND, THIS YEAR

1

Mt. Pisgah is in The Bible,
somewhere. Boxed up at home I have
a bible, in a box of its own.
My grandmother gave it to me.
She is dead. I am in England.

I lived on Mt. Pisgah once, not
the one in The Bible. When I lived
on my Mt. Pisgah, I didn't
know The Bible had one. I was
young, I guess. But I lived there.

Now that I know The Bible has
a Mt. Pisgah, I feel better
about The Bible. Though I bet
they never skied there. Grandmother
made us hold hands when we said grace.

And sent me most of *The Complete
Writings of Emerson,* before
she died. In my family, I
get the books, like the boxed Bible.
Though where the rest of Emerson

is, I'd like to know. Probably
boxed up in America somewhere.
Like grandmother. I think of death,
sometimes. Though the closest I've come
to a corpse is you. I think of you

like a mountain I lived on once
and later found in an old book
about prophets and locusts. It was
great grandfather's. I never touched
him, only his hard black scribble.

II
The rope lay still between the ruts,
and the hill rose into darkness
as the lights came down. Then home
through the heavy trees and the last
silences I can remember,

neither my own breathing nor soft
hiss of snow on steel edges.
In the morning, if I was first,
I could rip it out of its crust
like a beef-string, bobbing upward.

And at dusk, the light slid westward
under a quick lava, leaving
Whiteface in sunlight, its gaunt cross
crooked as rock, and the juke box
blasting out of the warming shack.

III
Who called it Pisgah because they
saw God, and the cross on Whiteface
made it palpable. Who they were,

neither Sunday school nor teacher
cared or seemed to know or found out.

Nor have I, though I think of them.
I lived on the lower meadows
of their dream, ignorant of them.
Though now that I'm twenty years gone
myself, treading the still waters

of a faith I think I once had
and a life that now seems at an end
or is changing in ways that I
can't fathom, I think of them, hard.
I think of them till my brain aches.

IV
Hanna Bairstow, wife to John Bray,
John Anthony Bray, who was sent
by Thomas Young, whether teacher
or friend is not known, *The Oeconomy
of Human Life,* as gift, inscribed.

September 1843,
leaves in their first descent, John Bray
soon to be married or perhaps
there already, Hanna in lace
laughing, and the years beginning.

Published, London, 1806.
Sent to me, sitting in England,
as Mamoo (Mary Bray) breaks up
her house after eighty-five years
(where was a farm, a highway grown),

with instructions to throw it
in the trash should I not want it,
who slept with an empty pistol
under her pillow, called me "Sweet Toad"
till I was thirty, and never

married. Oeconomy, indeed.
Whose brother, Thomas, Uncle Tom,
skirmished with the church and lost,
preferring, instead, a life still
as house-air in the driven dust,

who cackled when he laughed, "trays beans,"
looked like Thomas Stearns Eliot,
and kept us all locked in his head.
From whom I took these notes the last
time he said I'd see him alive.

He was right. Oeconomy. Now,
you must go to a home, and wait,
who lived your whole life in one house.
One house. Molly has a teacher,
this year, who reminds me of you.

V

Across the valley, the mountains
still have their blunt tips in sunshine.
Whiteface particularly. Snow
highlights the cross I once thought
Longfellow made his poem of.

I never read it till I left.
Nor Emerson's, about fishing,
which I didn't finish. Cooper
I knew, and the Winslow Homer
watercolors hung by the stairs

in another house. None of this
mattered then, and even now is
almost laughably irrelevant.
Except that it happened. It has
mattered, somehow, to have been caught

up in something unmomentous,
the death of Uncas, an almost
forgotten sonnet, these mountains
which, if they bear our highways, bear
also our invisible will.

It is unlikely, ever,
that we will live here. That we have,
is a secret these mountains keep
to themselves, like a book boxed up
at the end of a life, unread.

HAM AND EGGS

I have to say this to myself,
as though I might forget.
I have to think about it: I
want to be happy.
I say that to the snow at my feet
as I cross the parking lot: I only
want to be happy.
But I must open this door first
since what I also want
is a cup of coffee
and a piece of apple pie.
I put my poems down on the counter
and let them worry about themselves for a while.
And I think about someone my age
saying what I just said out loud
in the snow where no one can hear.
It seems too small a load
for all these years to bear.
Roger Mitchell wants to be happy.
I can hear one of the old waitresses
who has given up trying to be young anymore,
who wears her slacks loose and comfortable,
her hair chopped, and no make-up,
who jokes with young Gino over the counter
about his army physical,
who prayed for him,
who tells him to cough

and then coughs herself way down inside
laughing at her own joke,
who calls herself loudly over the shoulder
one of the dirty old women.
I can hear her hollering it back to the kitchen,
my terrible secret.
She yells it like the usual thing,
just like that.

from IN A MEANTIME

*

It is time to stop trying to
remember which emotion one
was trying to have or avoid
on the night before Christmas when
one was six after Pearl Harbor.

Let us consider the beauty
of forgetting and of being.
Wherever you are tonight,
the small radios of the past
are crackling like burnt paper.

*

These times are like the rest, they said.
So give us joy, or silence.
In five minutes they were banging
on the door, their knuckles bloody.
More bandages, more wine, they cried.

*

Peace in Vietnam. I was ten when
that happened first. Only we called
it victory. We went out on
John Eubanks' front porch and shot a
gun. I'd never shot one before.

*
The old intolerable balance.
My brother dies but, ah, a rose
grows. My brother does not die, he
is prevented. By these housewives,
these car buffers. Even from death.

He is slaughtered and a rose grows.
He is opened and it makes
no difference. He is worn, once. He falls
apart so we can keep our breath
fresh for freedom and the next fuck.

A Clear Space on a Cold Day (1986)

HOMAGE TO BEATRIX POTTER

I

I do not know a lot about Beatrix Potter,
but if she were my daughter,
I would tell her not to bother, so much,
about good behavior.

I would wonder what I had done to her
and under what pretext
to have been turned into a Macgregor
for her Peter to anger.

And in a garden, over an issue like property.
And in the company of imploring
but otherwise quite useless sparrows.
Life was difficult in the nineteenth century.

But I don't think mothers, even then,
sent their sons to the usual slaughter
with a chuck under the chin
and a wry word about potted father.

And then went out to buy five currant buns,
including one for their errant son,
who might or might not, according to the whim
of dread, come home again.

I think of the mouse with her mouth full of pea
who stopped to gag something kind
but incomprehensible, and the cat
who twitched at the bright orange fish in the pond.

And the hob-nailed boots that kicked
through the potted plants, and the raised rake,
and the tiny rage at the little rabbit
whose only habit was eating.

I wonder if minding mother would ever matter
in a world of Macgregors, and others,
who like to see some things grow,
but not others.

II
I am the father of Peter Rabbit.
I was eaten by Mr. and Mrs. Macgregor on Sunday
after being skinned in the tool shed,
boned in the kitchen,
and boiled for several hours in a metal pot.
Mr. Macgregor said I was good.
Mrs. Macgregor wasn't sure,
thought I was a bit stringy in places.
I was caught in the French beans,
a rake point driven through my skull.
I lived to be an example to my son.

III
It was the drawings I remember most,
the careful cabbages and a radish
that Peter seemed to pick his teeth with,
the tiny slipper in the dirt, and always

everything about to melt into the page
like snow fallen on clear water, two versions
of the same thing merging, a bright inhuman
whiteness, a small world paling into it,
like animals pretending to be people,
an invisible barrier disappearing,
an unimaginable brotherhood
of living things, as a book stands between
nothing and the person reading it.

THE LIFE I AM LIVING

It is a wild, rank place, and there is no flattery in it.
—Thoreau

Walking home alone at night,
I see myself as always walking
home alone at night. The wind
walks a cloud across the sky
on a light leash. The moon trembles.
A light goes on somewhere across
a street or yard. I am going
home, the place I left in haste
an hour ago. I couldn't wait
to leave. I was home alone,
and everything was home alone,
the windows, the plates, the things I knew.
The things I knew were there, always,
so I went out and the warm spring
evening that lay between the room
I went to and the house I left
put its arm across my shoulder.
There, it said, smiling, There, there.
Spring would not be unkind,
though I had heard it said, often.
I heard voices, mothers calling
into the dusk, children, muffled,
calling back. They would go home,
this time, and maybe the next,
but they were crouched next to the bush,

whispering: Wait, wait for me here.
I would go home, too, though to what,
I was not sure. Maybe the plates
or the spoons or the steep stairs.
But first I would walk through the trees
to a windowless room high on a hill,
high as the trees, which look that way
because branches, they say,
must not touch one another.
The wind thinks otherwise.
I think otherwise, too. I think
this is not my life, this mulling.
This is not me, not what I meant
when I said it is a wild, rank place.
I look in the lighted windows.
I listen to the sparkling gab
everywhere, the chatter and drone.
I turn it down like a radio
late at night. I keep it by me.
That is me talking of stars.
That is me taking the world by the hand
and leaving. I shall sit by the sea
and read. I shall look in the book
as I would a window, passed at dusk,
hoping to find there the life,
the one I am living.

HERE COMES HISTORY

Here comes history, everything blinking
and flashing, insisting that it can sit
on the horn all day, drive down the wrong side
of any issue it likes, knock the cart
full of carefully piled oranges into the street,
scattering the good gray people of the town
as though we were so much hen dust.
Where is the preacher, the doctor, the good
grim killer we hired to harbor the law?
Is he the one at the wheel, or is he
the one lashed to the stretcher in back,
writhing and dying before he arrives?

SCHOOL DREAM

I had gone back to the old brown rambling school
with its ancient test tubes, where I wanted to speak
and the person I wanted to speak with was never there
or had just stepped out. They knew me there, or it seemed that way,
though there were girls there now. One of them said hello,
and she and her friends clustered around me, laughing.
I did not feel as old as I was, as the teachers
who occasionally threw their older and knowing eye
like a pall across my suit. It was not new, I admit,
but it was clean. I needed a room, an inexpensive room,
to write my book in. I needed a little space,
and the food didn't have to be wonderful,
and if in a way it could be like a place I had known,
if it could be like that hopeful moment when I was poised
before the cruel errors that would make me the dreamer
surrounding himself with beautiful knowing older girls
who thought he was something, or with the long corridors
and dark paneling of the school that allowed him
to be important and smart and play football
to everyone's amazement, he was so skinny and afraid,
if it could be like that for a while, two or three months,
I might write the book I wanted to write,
as soon as I could remember what it was about.
But I could remember what it was about later
when I had the room and the bed and the small table
in the corner and the lamp and the meals brought to me,
which needn't be anything fancy, and the woods

to walk in and the occasional girl smiling at me
and the teachers who knew more than they told
keeping their distance, letting this happen because
they knew what it was and knew that someday
they would need to go back to an old rambling past
that had never happened and were secretly cheering
for themselves as they drudged past with their wisdom
and folders, sagged from having been held too long
and rearranged and written everywhere into the margins.
It was the teachers I was afraid of, it was the teachers
who knew too much, more than they wanted to know,
it was the teachers who bore the tell-tale marks,
the tiny scars that no one sees, who had been good at hiding,
and cheering us on at the edge of the field or the end
of the corridor under the light marked "Exit."
They were the dreaming adults we swore we wouldn't become,
who kept us away from home and the world and ourselves.

CINDERELLA

I

When they found her prostrate in the garden,
talking to a beetle, they locked her in the loft.

There it was spiders. For them, she danced
and made strange noises in her throat.

Nothing could shame her. Tied to the hog trough,
she wallowed in mud and warm moonlight.

At dawn, a sow lay sleeping against her.
She hugged a tree, and they took her clothes away.

She tried to nurse a calf, so they killed it.
And then wiped their hands on her naked breasts.

She would leave all this someday. But for now
she kept to the barn, mooing in the stillness.

II

When she left, she put a tear in a sack
and left it by the back door. It was dawn.

The frog in her palm collected itself
and leapt over the gate.

She would leap like that if she had to.
She would be the fox if the dogs came near.

She followed the ant and the low shrub,
and carried a knife now to bite with.

III
The sisters, naturally, were beautiful.
And, naturally, they were described otherwise.

She knocked on the back door, twice, begging for food.
They stared at her caked thighs, her ropey hair.

One of them threw her a shoe, the other
a cinder, and then watched as she choked them down.

They smiled their smiles in the right places,
but behind the barn they took cats apart.

The boys in the village, though, hung out their tongues
and dreamt. And some of them wept, and some cursed.

She was a broom dressed as a shawl, crouching.
Into her life crept nothing, breathing.

IV
He was not a prince. He was not even rich.
He was a woodcutter, and he drank.

There was no ball, there was no slipper,
and the clock had not yet been invented.

Someone else would think of these things:
the princes and the glass-like elegance,

the indoor bliss and the irreversible
severance from everything living,

the impossible splendor,
life in an up-thrust, thick-moated tower.

She wept at the woodcutter's death,
but dug the grave herself, the same day.

She never went back. She didn't need to.
Birds flittered over the new grass. The moles hummed.

NOW

Now, and in the face of all bearable
obstacle and impediment, and without
benefit of sanctifying or
otherwise corroborating theory
or device, free of all haunting visions
and insecurities of mind, open
as much to the spider's drool as to
the implacable stone and shadowed marvel
of the hours, in full cognizance and reach
of the huge black wind blowing through our bones,
the needled sperm lash and the pus-born wish,
with throat extended and deep hypnotic hum
as of armies swarming, in daylight born
and in the darkness born once more, alone
but with those I love now close about me,
I, Roger, abstract speck upon the void,
reeking with wild and half immaculate
satisfaction, do hereby state and make,
in the numbed presence of my enemies,
the worm, the laundry, and the arch-fiend greed,
a cloak of pure conflicting rhetorics,
a gaudy panoply of smirks, a yip,
that that indifferent brute boo-ha in me
should not go naked or, what's worse, unseen.

THE LITTLE TABLE

I don't know where to begin this poem.
I don't know what to make it say.
I am not worrying, for the moment,
about the number of syllables in the line.
There are as many syllables as there are.
I will not refuse to admit any of them.
The least of them may be the key,
the most inconsequential and expendable article.
I am alone with my language,
the whole of it. It begs me to say
the simplest and most difficult things,
without intervention, without artifice.
When I tell it that it will not live forever that way,
it has a fit in the hallway.
It breaks the little table there, the one
that seems to have no function and is brown.
I do not know what you call it. It is very little.
And now it is broken.

THROUGH A CLOSED DOOR

I remember hearing my mother cry.
It wasn't much more than a small sob,
like a cat rolling over and stretching,
a hinge on a dry day, or table leg dragged.
But I didn't know mothers cried, then.
It was something babies did. Or sissies.
I must have thought that, when you grew up,
everything was all right, that you were fixed,
at last, like a clock or a pair of skis.
It was when I heard my mother cry,
from another room, through a closed door,
that I began to wonder.
                            I began to wonder
what else I didn't know that I thought I knew.
Did everything keep secrets? Did the snow
fall only to rise again? Was that the tree
talking back when you stepped on the stair?
Was hair a kind of water that your hand,
a five-tongued mouth, drank, lapping it back?

On the day that my mother tried to hide
her feelings, she gave me mine.

for the children at U.S. Grant School, Sheboygan, Wisconsin

THE TWO SECRETARIES

Yesterday, I was distracted by the waiter.
You had just said something about men
and first marriages when he stuck his arm
between us. He stuck his arm between us
several times. Thick plates clattered in back of us.
It was that part of the restaurant
and that part of the day. I said nothing then
of the two young women sitting next to us,
the one on my side closer to me than you.
Though it was secretly their conversation
I was listening to. No one could have guessed.
Not even you, who have had to put up with
my faulty attention longer than you'd like to.
They talked about Jews and Catholics.
They talked about Protestants. They were wondering
who was what at the office, and why.
"If you're not Jewish or Catholic," said the one
closer to you, the one whose face I avoided
looking into, "you must be Protestant."

The cracked plate shone under the cannelloni.
It was their own world they were digging up,
bits of it glinted with thought.
One of them was Black, so I thought of my daughters.
"I think of you every day," I told them
in the second year of the divorce. I hoped,
I suppose, that thinking might keep them from harm
or the dozen small things this side of harm.

Let me say this once, and then be done with it.
The day I drove them away, Molly was still.
I could hear the pistons thumping in the block.
Bridget broke into sobs that she couldn't stop.
I had driven their mother to the edge of town
months before and left her next to a truck,
a U-Haul truck with a bright wide band around,
and in it the nicked chairs and the sad bed.
I think we shook hands. We may have said thanks,
or good luck.

I think of them not many years from now,
saying to someone somewhere in a sure voice,
"Catholics go to mass" or "Jews are not
Protestants," putting the ruin together
again, most of which I have forgotten
to tell them about, though not all. And so,
have added to their innocence and,
I can almost believe, to the gradual
elimination of the past, the best of the past,
I realize, but also the worst.

What we did with the rest of that day tumbles
into memory, though I think it was then
that we stood before Titian's "Man in a Red Cap,"
at Seventieth and Fifth Avenue.
Whose slightly flared hair and vulnerable lean
toward the frame, exciting the English ladies
behind us, told us in twenty seconds or so
why that merchant democracy, once Othello's,

could not bear the weight of itself, but fell
into the mazy streets and clean stones
we went half way round the world to see.

THE STORY OF THE WHITE CUP

for Helen

I am not sure why I want to tell it,
since the cup was not mine, and I was not there,
and it may not have been white, after all.
When I tell it, though, it is white, and the girl
to whom it has just been given, by her mother,
is eight. She is holding a white cup to her breast,
and her mother has just said good bye, though those
could not have been, exactly, the words. No one knows
what her father has said, but when I tell it,
he is either helping someone very old with a bag
or asking a guard for a cigarette. There is, of course,
no cigarette. The box cars stand with their doors
slid back. They are black inside, and the girl
who has just been given a cup and told to walk
in a straight line and to look like she wants
a drink of water, who cried in the truck
all the way to the station, who knew, at eight,
where she was going, is holding a cup to her breast
and walking away, going nowhere, for water.
She does not turn, but when she has found water,
which she does, in all versions of the story, everywhere,
she takes a small sip of it and swallows.

KEENE VALLEY, LATE FALL, STARSET

Standing in the meadow above the rush of the unseen river,
dusk, and the air gray along the edges of the west mountains,
the leaves half fallen and the rest turned yellow-brown,
the air cool and getting cooler quickly, the sky clear,
clear the way sky that has been clear all day is clear,
and the one star in the whole sky above the nearest mountain
setting, and trying to wish quickly, the way I was taught,
secretly, before the second star appears, before the blink,
standing in the open meadow, the huge house moored behind me,
its one light casting itself thinly across the grass,
across the now deserted garden scattered with compost and ash.
And not knowing, finally, what to wish for. And so,
not wishing at all, but standing there watching a star move.

Adirondack (1988)

KNOW YE THAT WE

of our right forever
                    fully
and freely for a sum
of money
              absolutely
and fully
and forever
                for ourselves
and our Nation forever
at a Publick meeting
                        fully
and freely
and absolutely
              +
grant, Bargain, sell,
release, convey, infeoff,
Cede, dispose of, surrender
                              forever
              +
all tract & Tracts,
all parcel & parcels,
all Quantity & Quantities

and also all
                and singular
the Trees
                and also all

the Woods
and Underwoods,

the Rivers, Streams, and Ponds,
the Creeks, Rivulets, and Brooks,
                                    and Runs,
              all and each
        +
              as well as all
flowages and seepages else,
droplets of moisture,
accumulations of dew,

for which neither we
nor the drafters of this deed
can find name,
        +
the land which underlies the land
and that which underlies that land,
                                and all,
        as deep as may be reached,
        +
water that shall fall from the sky,
drizzle or deluge,
                        air,
motionless or not,
which shall lie on this land
        or pass across it
or cross and recross it,
                        at whatever pace,

according to its whim,
                          up
even to the furthest reach of the eye,
                    and beyond,
            +
the light
and the dark

and all gradations between them,
                                        dusk
and dawn,

and before them and after them both,

the light at midsummer's midday, cloudless,

midwinter's midnight,
moonless,
        +
and the animals that walk thereon,
of whatever sort and variety,

the clumsy, swift-legged moose,
the remotest vole,

the beaver, the panther,
the beetle,

those that burrow,
                        however deep,

those that fly,
                    however high,
or far,

so long as they shall return,
        +
all manner of thing
                    forever,
all aspect or quality,
all attribute
                or way,
fully
     and freely,
        +

                so that
in time to come
when we are asked for,
they will not know
what word to use.
        +

Hendricks, alias Tayahansara   Mark.
Lourance, alias Agwiraeghje
Hans, alias Canadajaure   Mark.
Johans Crim, alias Onagoodhoge,

        we
        of the Mohock Castle

In 1772 representatives of the Mohawk Indian tribe sold over
a million acres of land in northern New York to white land
speculators for 1135 pounds "lawful Money of New York."

AFTERNOON AT THE GUIDE MUSEUM

not so much a lover of nature as a part of nature
                    —Charles Dudley Warner

Don't let the soiled, stubby, bow-legged thrust
fool you. This one was much sought after,
subject of essays, often visited.
This other lived in a bark shack with his dogs,
hunted—though not for the meat (which he ate),
nor for the love of uncanny skill (which he had)—
is said to have killed the last moose in the state.
This one had five children, a wife,
got "howling" drunk whenever he could.
One day he stopped, and he stopped for good.
This one wrote verses and never bathed.
This one was painted by Winslow Homer
next to this other, though neither was named.
This one was known to have beaten his wife
and was almost taken to court. This one
played violin. Not fiddle, but violin.
This one led Benedict Arnold to Canada,
this other Burgoyne toward Saratoga.
Neither appeared in the dispatches
nor was afterward blamed for the defeat.
Most of them came here from other places—
Scotland, Vermont—though this one was Indian.
That paddle he holds was his real paddle.
This one was known for his way of saying
a single word, the word was "well."

This one put John Brown's body into its grave,
where, as the song tells us, it moldered.
This one was seen once, flat on his face,
hugging a mountain. "I'm with you again,"
he was heard to whisper.

This last one, no one remembers.
He is the most popular one in the exhibit,
the one people touch. He is the one
who, in the photograph, can't be identified,
who stands off at the edge of the picture,
a saddle of venison slung like a yoke
over his shoulders and neck, who was asked
to stand still for a moment, and did,
but who couldn't, or wouldn't, look
straight into the future, at you and me,
whose name, though not for that reason,
or so we assume, has been lost or forgotten,
but whose slight, muscular body—
not quite in focus, on cracked paper,
in a picture taken by someone else
we can't identify, almost thrown away—
shows us the unease of a man hired.
Though some prefer to see in the dropped chin,
the furtive eyes, the look of a man looked at,
seen, of a man who would rather have been—
like the animals he stalked—unseen.

Perhaps one of you recognizes him,
the uncle whom no one mentioned, who knocked

on the back door late one night in a snow storm,
who handed in part of a bear, but was not
going to be asked in, and knew it, and so
stamped his feet in the doorway once and left.
Or the one you invented, the father
who spent the rest of his life looking
for the child he gave away. You see him
in every man you meet, looking for the child
you still are. The back of your mind collapses
like a rotted wall. Inside, a tiny,
mute swarm of memories writhes in the light,
slithers into the darkness.
Bent particles float through your eyesight.
You remember light bursting or water
surrounding you. On the day you knew
you were here forever, you slept that night.

THE PADDLE

There are no memoirs,
no letters or diaries,
no lists, no hand-
scrawled maps to the next
cabin or pond,
no signatures
on mortgages,
no bit of clothing,
old boot or sock,
no bottle to which once
he put his mouth,
no lock of hair,
scissor to cut with,
knife to skin bear,
gold watch or fob,
likeness of other,
tooth of the panther,
moose jaw,
lip-blackened pipe.

The photographs give us
the bulk of the body,
the wrinkled face. But,
faces are everywhere.
Bodies abound.
Who has made his face
as this was made?

Who has chosen
a look, as the wood
of the right tree
was chosen, the line
of the grain? Who
has shaved speech,
or thought, as this blade
was shaved? Who has smoothed
the skin of the body,
darkened it
with its own oil?

This paddle, long,
squared at the end,
narrow, its handle
a T for good
gripping, a tree reduced
to a way
of being—thin,
springy, light—
of turning
as the elements
turn, in their flow,
or against them
if need be,
finding the narrow
seam in the air,

feathering
the leaden water,
the self, hidden,
though not from itself,
guiding itself, lulled,
at the world's edge
over the quick
falls, beside
the dark woods.

from THE MONOLOGUES OF
VERPLANCK COLVIN

*Colvin was for many years the official surveyor of the Adirondacks.
A theodolite was especially useful to surveyors because it could
measure angles both horizontally and vertically.*

1898

The night we burned a mountain by mistake,
the men quivered setting their packs down.
Who had no more food, the deer startled off
by our scrambling through unbroken forest,
burdened with gear. Vernier calipers,
rods, chains. The delicate theodolite,
its box and harness. Three hundred pounds
stretchered like a sultan or a sultan's
pet wife, like creamy Cleopatra, over
gorge and precipice, through swamp and windslash.

I think of that. Of that alone, sometimes.

And the men. I don't know why they did it,
those who did, those who didn't stalk off cursing
through the snow. They cheered. In the freezing gales
they cheered, when I marked and read and reread four times,
to be sure, and wrote down in the great ledger,
in a slowed hand, the last point on Marcy.
How could they not cheer. Here, the earth unravelled,
cold, remote, treeless at its peak. And now,

we knew its height above Paris, London,
even the pyramids, the scuttled barge,
above her calm, wrapped body.

UNDATED ("I never gave a thought")

I never gave a thought to those who quit.
Captains have been set adrift before.
All wars have their deserters. Why not mine?
I fought mine against what did not seem
possible, what they said could not be done.
That they were right means nothing. To have tried,
that I will take to my grave, happily,
if there is to be one. Though to be found
lying on the floor of some hotel lobby,
mutinied by my own breath, seems more likely.

Yes, that was me muttering through the grime
of back street Albany in 1912.
I was thinking of Burgoyne's army
(another soldier set adrift near here),
of boys from Bedfordshire and Rutland.
I could almost hear the flat whack of the axe,
the crackle of falling trees, the curses,
as the road nosed forward, as the great trees
died. I think of the wormy bread and cheap rum
in the bellies of those boys, of the hope
they must have had for a quick fight, clean wound,
anything to get them on the ship back home.

Though I see one stoop and pick up a clod
of duff and crumble it through his hands.

You can still see bits of the road, or could,
logs laid out like corpses after battle.
Blaze marks, too, still visible on trees,
not many, but a few. A pile of stones
where someone thought his wanderings would end.
Dead clearings, fields gone back to forest.
Ring bolts on mountaintops, sunk in rock.

UNDATED ("A thing like a map")

A thing like a map left unfinished
is always to be done. I left my life
as I found it, here, so it would not end.
And it didn't. It disappeared instead.
I have been studying the way things stop
recently, how there is rarely a warning,
how it has almost always happened
already, as when we wake up one morning
and, though the sun shines and it is warm, summer
is over, and also how everything
should have forewarned us, how there was death
in everything we did, long, slow strolls
through the summer dusk, and how, if a thing
can't be pure at the start, a true leap,
it can't be—can it?—at the end, an end.

UPRIGHT AND FALLEN

There is an impassive, stolid brutality about the woods,
that has never been enough insisted on.
              —Charles Dudley Warner

The featureless bland faces of Homer's boy hunters, impassive
as in watching with equanimity and disinterest the work
of their own hands, the log laid low or the hand-made knife
as its blade passes in gray light under the terrified throat,
stolid as in doing the thing doggedly, as in thinking this
is the only way, the boy-like innocence of the boy, foot cocked
on the stump, the dogs baying at the hide draped easily
over the barrel of the rifle which itself rides loosely
across the shoulder of the boy who gazes, or if not gazes,
lifts his face into the air, glazed with sunshine and sweat.

So that, without moving, as though by trick of the eye,
the boy joins the things he stands among, disappearing
among the leaping and draped forms, the upright and fallen,
blood-spattered browns, mud-shaped swales, glint and froth.
It is all one and sundered, and nothing comes back whole
but comes, if at all, like the fawn seen nibbling, quickly,
or the child full of distance it still hasn't traveled.
The gentlest wrist, blood threading its bones, is cruel,
the tree standing there and the weeds looking for light.
I have hated a stone for being there, for being a stone.

The Word For Everything (1996)

YOU'RE HERE

and despite all the tricks of dis-
placement and slid syntax,
despite all you know of the need
the mind has to be elsewhere,
or the greased border between world
and the words that would say they
were the world, you know where you are.
I know. I should be talking
in images. I should be over there.
But I'm here, and though it's a place
with a name and a kind of look
to the hills and the way rocks
break through the skin of the earth
exposing the bones,
and the people seem relentless,
I can still stand at the corner
of First and Woodlawn and feel
what I've always felt, at all
the corners: a part of the wind.
The wind that right now at the end
of August refuses to move,
that last year snapped the Lombardy Poplar,
that carries the ash and the dust,
that brings the sighs and the sirens,
the curses, right into the living room,
last repository and resting place
for all the last words and the last

strangled breathings, that must be,
or enter, the bird's anatomy,
that must be, or resemble, a sea,
or the currents of that sea,
in which we do, if we do,
the singular swim, the long
slippery slope, of being here.

BORROWING HENRY

The little essay on the ant creeps forth
on the assumption that someone—Jim, let us say—
listens. Jim is not obliged to listen,
and to judge from the blank days in the journal
and the perfectly wooden passages,
which Henry, of course, would think improved
for resembling the xylem and phloem,
Jim wanders off at times, no one knows where.
Jim is the reason Henry hurries back
from Conantum. Jim is the reason
he sits up late with a candle or lamp
and thinks about two hawks. Jim, he would say,
and he would tell him something odd. And Jim
would say, "that's odd," the way Henry wanted,
or Jim might nod or gaze at the ceiling.
And Henry, remembering each detail,
would tell how the tightly compacted fawn
falls out of its mother, almost like shitting,
the nose pressed down between the two front feet,
the doe twisting to get her body right
and tossing her head back to look, sniffing
the new birth. This, he would say, and then stop.
He would think of the smell of the body.
Jim, he would say. But Jim would be gone by then.
It was a marvel. He could be right there
in his room thinking, Jim in the corner,
the lamp filled and the wick trimmed down.

Then he'd be gone, into the body, say,
into the body of a doe, his nose
pressed flat between his hands, a terrible
convulsion thrusting at him, squeezing him,
and when he thought his ribs would crack, and the whole
sky shove into his chest at once, the air
licked him, stood shaken above him, sniffing.

CLANG

A woman stands in a cornfield at the end of day.
Nowhere does the "extensive totality of life"
bear down with such menace as in southern Indiana.
These are not just rocks by the side of the road.
It is not just a pleasantness of trees
that gathers here. The man out back
raises a maul above his head and brings it down
with enough force to change the course of a life.
It is the straight green grain of black locust,
and like a good life it sings when it's split.

The leaves come down off the trees in the fall,
and there's a moment near dusk when you don't know
if it's the last of the swifts racing
for its hole or the first uncertain bat
launching its night-long raid on the bug life,
which may be the true life, of this wrinkled
republic, this land careening down a hill
of river bottoms, ox bows, limestone and mud.

MUSIC I KNEW

It was in Katowice, I think, in Silesia,
where the Polish border officials
in their snug uniforms of olive brown
boarded the trains going south into Czechoslovakia.
We were swarmed over in minutes by gypsies
going home for Christmas, assuming
that gypsies have a home, and Christmas.
Each year at that time those from the mines
and factories of southern Poland
go south into Czechoslovakia, and on,
I was told, into Hungary where gypsies,
briefly, cease being themselves and settle down.

Across from me the woman with no teeth
and black shining eyes had seven skirts
which she lifted like a bundle of laundry,
a handful of curtains, in search of a passport,
when the smiling border official slammed
the glass door back and shouted in seven languages
at once, none of them gypsy, "Passports, please."
Mine lay on my lap, the blank page turned.
The little gypsy girl, who also had seven skirts,
each for a time in her life when she would cease
being the person she was and start
being someone else, dodged among them
with a plastic bag full of passports,
collecting and dispensing at random,

to all her brothers and sisters, to all
her mothers and fathers, one jump ahead
of the trim border officials whose duty
to protect the state from disorder is hard,
who keep their minds on their high, clear task
and stamp with a small spring-loaded stamp,
eventually, whatever is laid before them.

I think it was that night, later,
after the gypsies had risen at Prague
in a body and burrowed into the darkness,
steam swirling along the platforms,
in search of a train that would take them
back into Hungary. Though who would have room
in Hungary to house these hundreds, with their skirts
and their bags full of fresh kohlrabi,
which they cut with a wide-bladed knife
on the thick flat pad of their thumbs
and eat in the same closed compartment as you
offering you some, too, which you take
and say, thank you, I come from America,
I live in a house, the night is cold.

It was then, that night,
when the gypsies were gone, when the spunk
and the sharp smell of kohlrabi stayed on
with the long sinews of tribes and the songs,

which we have only learned to disguise,
as we crept toward Vienna and Rome,
that the family from somewhere in central Europe got on.
And all night, as we rattled south toward the border
or waited, murmuring, on unlit sidings,
were slammed out of something like sleep
by several smiling officials, as our passports
were looked at and stamped and looked at again,
I watched, in the dim light, under the lid of sleep,
the mother, the father, two daughters, a son,
drink something clear from each other's glances.

It was a hot, cramped compartment on a train
crossing central Europe twenty years ago.
It was a night full of slammed doors and songs
sung in the back of my throat, as I slept
or pretended to sleep, as I crept forward
toward Vienna and Rome, the rest of my life,
listening to a music I had never heard, but knew,
a song I would come to sing, already mine.

REMEMBER

I remember going somewhere in a car.
Black shadows gathered
under some trees. That was the way
things happened then. Afternoon.
A large house by a lake.

It must have been Lake George.
Up the west side somewhere near
Bolton Landing. I don't know why
I know that. We were there
for the afternoon, I don't know

why or for how long. I just remember
shadows milking the trees,
the brooding of a large house
at the edge of them, and beyond it,
a shimmer of water.

I go back to this memory
from time to time, wondering
what it was, whether anything other
than shadows and a large house
beside a lake brought us there,

wondering what, if anything,
happened, and why, whether anyone
remembers why shadows gathered
and fell, sank into the ground,
whether anyone remembers anything.

What did that afternoon belong to?
To us? The memory of us?
What were the shadows and the trees,
and we, gathered there to do?
I was too small to know, four or five.

Yet I am the one still there,
standing by the lake and the dark hovering
next to it, the house I recall
nothing of but its wide summer porches,
and the watery lake beside it.

Maybe something in the word beside.
Maybe the heaviness of the trees.
It was closer to me, I suppose,
than the others, whoever
the others were, and made me see

the darkness, that it grew
next to houses, and above them,
that you could be beside a house
and in it, that you could pull
black trees around you, and the lake.

That all of this would disappear,
the reason and the people, the house,
but the darkness and the lake
would not, that we would become
these things, that we were already,

that it would take a lifetime
to find and find a way to say it,
saying darkness to the trees,
shimmer to the lake, saying
somewhere, or, remember.

RETURN TO A SMALL TOWN

It is and isn't there. The movie house
erased by grass, the lives I used to live
replaced by others, or not replaced.
I look for names on signs, flip standing up
at a pay phone through rain-rumpled pages,
though it wasn't names I memorized, but cracks
in sidewalks, looks on passing faces.
Nothing fits the two aging women
(both of whom I may have danced with in the gym)
standing by the city's cement planter, talking
about someone's heart. Or the man thumbing his wrist
(the bulging vein pops quickly back in place)
behind the register. I agree. It's hot,
and no one's buying. He puts the T-shirt
in a bag, folds it, stops, folds it again.
He doesn't hear me say, I came from here.
Or does. Maybe that's what rummaging
among the day's receipts means. Maybe
that's what saying nothing says,
looking across the sagging racks of shirts
that no one wants, even at half price.

WHAT HAPPENS NEXT

We don't know what happens next in John Sloan's
5 x 7 etching, "Man, Wife and Child."
The man's suspenders dangle off his back.
Plump and still corseted, the wife leans
into him. And he leans back. They stand, hugging
each other hugely, holding the other's eyes
with a fond, playful lust which the child, dressed
in a loose jumper for bed, her head too large
for her body, her thoughts starting to beat
like a startled wren against the dresser, the chair,
the small framed print, the broad-bellied pitcher
in its bowl, finds almost wonderful.
She reaches out as if to join their dance,
a dance she almost knows the music to.
But these two upright wrestlers (the wife pulls—
she may be merely hanging on—at the back
of his collarless shirt opening) don't know,
for the moment, she's there, don't care. Though, of course,
they do. They live in a room together,
and the stiff collar stands like a sentinel
on the dresser, the tie, untied, still threaded
through it. Drawers stand open, a spoon slants
out of a cup, or is it a bowl, and the girl,
who came from something like this, and almost knows it,
who ought to be in bed, but isn't, sees
that tonight it doesn't matter, and won't
ever again. Her mother's forearm grips
the small of her father's back. It's 1905.
What happens next is nothing next to this.

STRONG COFFEE

Strong coffee going upstream, slow jazz
coming down. Unmistakable Milt Jackson,
the sun translucing his cool vibrato.
Praise John Lewis, that philosopher of the
interval, the one between the meaning
and the meaning, slow to break open the chord,
tireless in working out the calculus
of feeling. You come away loosened a little
along the fault line between the coastal
shelf you came from, waving its sinuous
underwater weed, and the crumbling range
of dust and hill you built your life on,
incipient mud slide, that cactus ranch
of choices made in the name of what
somebody's mother knew well led to hell's
spectacularly barnacled foyer. Oh yes,
whoever she was, she made it possible,
over and over, to be lifted. She brought
Johnny Hodges directly up out of the
bloodstream, stroking his velvet sax.
I learned my mambo because she knew,
but would not say, where it would lead.
But it led there, straight as whiskey
in a straw. I thank my mambo for what
she taught me with her silence. So what
if I got there just as the band broke out
in "Fugazzi's Blues." I got there.

SEGMENTS OF SPINE

A squashed bottle or torn bag
ground into the cinders by the roadside,
volcanic dust. We had come down the west
side of the island, through eucalyptus
and long-needled pine. The road
rolled over thick tendons of mountain,
the potholes and rocks loosening the car
from its own bolts. We turned east
onto a slope of old lava, black
and rust red, the scorch of original earth.
Spiked bushes in clusters, cactus,
the odd kiawe twisted up out of rock,
the occasional breath of a meadow—
a lung among all those bones—the sea
blue-purple and green beyond, wind stretched
tight across its belly. We parked the car,
a banged-up, off-white rental, the kind
now and again pushed into the guavas,
under the monkey pods, the hanging trumpets.
Or like the one we saw completely beached
on the rocks, stripped and beaten to a thin
skeleton of rust. We got out and stood
looking, now at the ground, the crushed bottle
or torn bag in the cinders, now downhill,
the mile or two it was to the coast, the six
or so it was beyond where the sea
turned to sky. But it was up into the rock

ravines we looked longest, arroyos, deep
creases in the slopes, which if your eyes kept
climbing, took you up declivities
you could only imagine, ledges even
the goats avoided, birds circled warily,
where mountain stopped and the flat underside
of cloud began. Later, we would come upon bones
in a small grove of kukui, lumbar
arrangements, pelvic scoops, scattered
segments of spine. Though I remember
the pig-shaped swarm of maggots laid
in the toothed shadow of a palm.
And once, clambering up a ridge,
startling the black, bearded billy of all
these gullies and his two current consorts,
one of whom, dragging a back leg, stumbled
and fell as they scrambled to get away,
stumbled again, stopped, and stood staring
at the rock in front of her. It seemed then
she might decide this was the place, the way
when the lion in the film finally
brings the Thompson's gazelle down, and before
its teeth meet each other in the neck,
the gazelle has gone to sleep. All day we climbed,
not caring where the folds in the landscape
took us. Once, through a maze of kiawe,
out onto rock ledges scored by the goats,
we came into a grove of thready limbs.
Two low caves thrust into a wall—
a cul-de-sac—of rock, reeking of cat,

fetor of pig. Clambering, we came out
onto the grazed bend in a ridge and stopped,
the wind carrying a small whinny down
from the cloudy portages above us.

I don't quite know what it means, if it means
anything, to climb down into the skull
of a dry creek, to run your hands along
the smoothed outer curve of water.
Cloud comes down and calm ravages the air.
We want to be where we are, but we can't
quite find it. You shout from the other side
of a ridge. You have almost broken loose,
gone past, but at the last possible gasp
of immensity, pull back, your face pale.
I want to go up into the cloud, you say,
but I want you to go with me.

FOUR HUNDREDTH MILE

I am 83 miles north of Indianapolis on I-65.
A few clouds are out and the corn stands
dead on its feet on either side of the road.
It is dusk and the light leaps up
to take its last look at the world.
It is September, early September, and the leaves,
though they feel the soft stroking of the air,
shiver slightly.
I am driving my four hundredth mile of the day,
alone now, and calm, the lights of the oncoming cars
beginning to sparkle in the dying light.
Huge flat-sided semis, as the night comes on,
pass like immense untroubled animals,
like the sides of houses in a flood.
How many times have I been here and not seen
the width of the sky, the slow curve of the landscape
going away, the tiny wire trailing after?

This is the place and this, undoubtedly, the way.
As much of the sky above as there can be,
as much of the earth beneath.
This is the place where the world appears
in its robe of night and day,
where the dirt road travels with us a ways
and then turns sharply along the ditch,
disappearing down interminable rows of corn.
This is the place where you can see forever,
where pure emptiness hangs on outspread wings
circling above a field.

The soul ranges everywhere and everywhere finds
what it needs, a stick, a fleck of matter on the tongue.
The bird at the top of the dead tree will fly
before I can see it, so I will see it fly.
The cow in the truckbed in front of me looks out
at the world and, if I'm not mistaken, sees it.
The car makes a steady wind-ripped thrum, the glow
of the dashboard rising into my eyes like dust.
I am somewhere between exits. The promising sign,
"Vacancy," flashes above trees in the distance.
I am in no hurry. The only thing in front of me
is home, a few stars, and another night.
I have tried to love what I thought was the world,
but the world moved. I will love the move instead.

THE WORD FOR EVERYTHING

There is the word for you
and beside it the word *me,*
though neither of us knows which they are.
There is the word for the two of us together
or apart. Together
and apart.
There is the word for chair,
the word *clear.*

There is the word for this moment, too,
though no one can pronounce it.
It is not now,
though there is the word *now,*
and the word *slow.*
Between them is the word
one does not hear,
the word these words look for,

here by the clear chair,
deep in the slow now.

Braid (1997)

BRAID

A poem that thinks its way toward itself, a poem
    beginning with
the letter "a," poem assuming the worst, as
    well as the best, that the purpose is lost
        but can be found, that it does not know itself
sufficiently,
    but can, that when it arrives there, trembling,

bleeding a little around the mouth, torn from itself,
    having survived
things it cannot, at the moment, know, since it knows
    no language adequate to its condition,
        pretending, as it has for centuries, it is
what it is not,
    is where it cannot be, poem equal

to the world, to the tree, to the fragments of graying
    styrofoam
stuck in the Sargasso Sea, or strung out along
    the fence with the wrappers and torn bags, crushed
        aluminum cans, possum carcasses, dried grass.
The swallow stops
    in mid-flight, then turns avidly bugward.

So we stand back a moment, flushed, unhook the harness
    of rhetoric

into which we too quickly strapped ourselves, into
    which we were too easily persuaded
        by ourselves, or those accumulated gestures
ringing in our
    ears. Of what? Do we need to say? Have we

words to say? What. What is it that lures us to the worm?
    What is it that
makes us want to roll all our strength up into one
    marvellous phrase or image, hoping to
        outtop time? Curious presumption, lingering
residue of
    theology. So opposed, say, to the cloud.

Opposed, too, to the intractability of things,
    aforesaid tree,
which no language knows but which all pay homage to,
    stumbling toward some approximation of
        the breeze, which now moves the leafed-out branches in a
slow, almost drugged,
    dance, though a dance in place. In Terlingua,

New Year's Eve, a cold moon pressing down on the dry earth,
    a string of lights
across the desert, red, a crowd of Mexicans,
    cowboys, a few Indians, old hippies,
        mothers, grandfathers, children, two dogs, plus a man,
paraplegic,
    out on the floor dancing with his torso,

twisting to the leaded beat, eyes screwed tight, arms
        waving a wind
we knew ourselves to be in but barely felt.
        Outside, the stars dripped down. The mountains rose
                in the distance, and the distance rose. We drove back
dreaming, the dawn
        dusting the dark, almost black, almost fixed,

sky. And then a train ride across Russia, a poem
        twelve translated
pages long. We drove down into the city and
        had lunch with several poets, editors,
                contentious writers of every variety
who turned and fled
        afterward back into their lives. It was

their lives that we could sense between phrases involving
        various things,
history perhaps or a particularly
        rough, not to say abusive, workshop. What
                did this one, who smoked all during lunch, go home to?
What was she there,
        who smiled, talked of her husband in futures

and kept pushing her hair back away from her face with
        a metal clasp,
while the young poet and editor told us John
        somebody was the best poet here (there)
                and asked if we wanted to hit (that was the word,
hit) the blues bars
        later that evening, to which we said, sure.

But didn't. The phone lay quiescent in its cradle
     all evening long.
Awake at five-thirty, birds now finished with their ac-
     knowledgments of dawn, territorial
          assertions, tunings of the syrinxes, wing fluffs,
I read a while
     and fall into a long stuporous sleep.

Poems, of course. Good, goodish, of a sort liable
     to be admired,
beginnings, endings, stanzaic arrangements mostly,
     words electrified by eccentrici-
          ty, sentences or their profligate, stand-up
substitutes, smack
     on the page like similes of tea stains,

but most particularly situations, human
     for the most part,
recognizable, sliced off the quivering, thick ham
     of immediate being-in-the-world,
          this latter thing of no use whatsoever, it
being the stuff
     of which the stuff is made, if stuff is made

and not assembled, squirted, whipped as into a froth
     or meringue, some
process we have no analogue for and hence no
     word. For. Car rumbles through the neighborhood
          thumping like a frog. There's music on the inside
but out here thump,
     a prowling, rhythmic declaration

of the groin. A thrust of black-eyed susans. Next to it,
  the garden fork.
We talked at breakfast. The words went back, but not forth,
  back further, back to their creaking homestead,
    complaint, uncertainty, resolution, fatigue.
We want to know
  what we know, and yet how easily

it eludes the part of us that would let us know it.
  Carolina
wren goes cheery in a bush out there. Last evening
  alone out at Beechwood Heights, brown thrashers
    banging in the underwoods, barn swallows skimming
over the grass
  beside the lake. Our place, our last pastime.

And yet I could summon no nostalgia for either.
  It was a place
we took our separateness to, let it walk around
  a little. Sonoma. Tart green apples,
    good only for cooking. Hot dry wind, sun playing
in the curved eu-
  calyptus leaves, spiny evergreen bush

against the fence. I could go on all day matching things
  to the few words
I have in my sack, none of it getting down to
  either the constructed beauty of small
    plots of owned land, fenced off from the rest of the world
or the small park
  where the old dreams lay in the grass and smoked.

I was there, briefly. Like a tourist copping a view.
    It was not good.
I was nervous. I was too well dressed. It was not
    the sixties, but the people had come there
        to be in the sixties. It was the form with no
content. It was
    poverty, destitution, the dirt blurred

and the mouthing of dead phrases. The world had gone
    by, leaving these.
So you do not have mountain or bluff above sea,
    remote valley or paradisal rock.
        You have this. You have this hour and its residue.
This sun on this
    lean of the day lilies, mouths kissing death.

You are in an airplane now, eating the strange items.
    Stewardesses
are pretty, often, and often they are not young
    anymore and have lived many lives and
        dealt with every kind of kindness, distress, rudeness.
And they go home
    somewhere at the end of the day, Pittsburgh,

maybe, or San Francisco. They walk through the airports
    in a perfect
calm, trailing their little wheeled bags, and find their ways
    back to that other world, predictable
        and surprising, old as the oldest thing, mountain
or pantomime,
    and as new as this year's crop of tiny

wild tart blueberries scattered on the outcropping.
    And ate, we said,
like bears. And came back from California, we said,
    like kites. And went into the restaurant,
        we said, like cantaloupes. Or into the bookstore
like bubblegum.
    We said this. We said into and like. Like

going into the room and seeing him lying there
    wrecked and weeping.
We were not prepared for this. We were ready but
    not prepared. We didn't stay long. We left,
        walked out into the hot dry air. Sebastopol.
Life intervenes.
    Months travel. Summer drags its flowered skirts

through the mud. Even the tamarack turns reddish brown,
    and the sky stays
a muted blue-gray for days. If nothing fits, wait.
    Ants swarm up my arm. White larvae writhe in
        the turned-over dirt. If nothing fits, nothing fits.
Months pass by. Days,
    slow-chapped and sodden. Hours like leaves just touched

by wind, carrying the thick wave of branch, the thin wave
    of leaf stem, both.
Minutes. There are minutes on the wall, seconds where
    a chair scuffed a jamb, lamb of memory
        rubbed, rubbed loose the plaster (I said, can you drive, can
you drive faster).
    Actually, she said that. No, I said.

No. A tree swallow works hard over the open field.
    I am down here
trying to understand the Jack-in-the-pulpit.
    It is like trying to understand sand
        or quantify certain moments when one (read "I")
knew that, but not
    how, I was going to get down the road.

So much has happened. Is it true that all poets see
    themselves as free,
controlling their medium and utterance? Well . . .
    Responsible only to the ages,
        the craft, no one, whatever suits the attitude
cultivated
    to flugelhorn essential, central stuff?

Model citizens, carrying their trays to the bay,
    as provident
as a banker, as bourgeois as an athlete trans-
    formed by his millions into supersales-
        person of the strive and jive economy. Green
in the new grass
    has a kind of gray in it that may be blue.

In Mary's paintings you can't see the underlayings
    of blues and reds,
except as a thickness or viscosity, just
    as in a face you can't see bones or in
        this beshrubbed suburb, the weed-killers (or the weeds),
the pocked highway,
    the poor, their poverty, your own neighbor.

Thirty-two. Almost everything I know, all my friends,
     whistle the tune,
let go. It's a tuneless tune. It has the rhythm
     of weather, never gets bored with itself.
          Whatever it is that doesn't like us to take
hold, pile one rock
     on another, arrange the nerve ends.

But who knows? Here's old reliable, still willing to
     think of reins, mark
out avenues and exits, color code the least
     flicker of brain warp, count the syllables,
          and generally fluff up the dust and make us feel
as though it's O
     K to steer your own rusty bobsled down.

When I heard it, I liked immediately the term,
     and it was in
a lecture, no less, wide room of upturned faces,
     the long marble or stone tablet required
          of the sciences, though this was a philosopher,
red-faced and full
     of the words of others, carrying the

(and this was his word) "conversation"—a word that has
     now entered our
conversation, its new all-purpose dashiki—
     forward. Forward and to the place thought lost
          forever. Remember forever? The tall doors,
floor-length curtains,
     the sea brushing our speech back tight against

our thought. The place where you could say that a thing was
    the thing it was. Well,
I'm no romantic, I, but I could swear I caught
    a glitter of crushed essentials, that slush
        of the stars brought up on the beach, and then raked back,
when "descriptive
    gravity" ("center of") broke and rolled in.

The skin may fall from the bone and the bone pulverize,
    the bone itself
come to museumize in Kankakee, where our more
    watery offspring glaze up at the thought
        that they descended from bone, had bone for breakfast,
but here it is,
    what we can only agree is the thing

we cannot agree on the verbalization of.
    Little essays
in paint. Garden, tumescent and gorged. Chard. The taking hold,
    rule and thumb, and making the stuck mule kick,
        four pages on how to build forms alone, the prose
plain, assertive,
    ideas sound, collard, good compost, beans.

It is why I like to dig. It is why, when I dream,
    plumeria
scattered on the asphalt. Or, the abandoned house
    riding its glacier of corn, or stuck
        up under the looped woodbine, draped wild grape, bindweed.
Morning glory
    wrapped around a pole. Shadow, eaten beam.

To take a rotted river, its cindered bank, bruised air,
    flower of East
Chicago, ornament of Calumet, Gary.
        Receding roofs, plumes of stacked blue slants, pipes,
            billows of smelter gas, roar, torn eyesight, blast, stink.
How can you not
    love what made this slash? It can unmake it.

What deep or deeper gash than this heaped-up crush of rent
    metal, down slope
glittering among spiny palms, uncombed cane, rush.
        Behemoth barnacled with rusted pipes,
            cam shafts, sprung axles, aerials bent and perplexed,
with blistered tires
    twisted out of its glass-spattered carcass.

A heap of language. A bush along the eroding
    low cliff of rock.
More sun than water, and more boredom than either.
        Waves churn up the sand, and a rain shaft drops
            into the blown water somewhere between there and
"heap of language."
        The waves shrug in, also jockeying to

be heap. Headlights, most of them broken, aimed everywhere.
    No comfort, not
even cloud come in over the sun's home, urgent
        caca, frittered effusions, laid along
            the edge of incremental sunlight. When I think
of being here
    and the long afternoons of blustery wind.

Breeze rattling the dry blades of the coconut palm,
 blue bask, cracked grass.
He came across the water low, lower than that,
 wheels almost nicking the tiny rippings
  of fetch. Description is never just the raw gashes
of red raked down
 the strafed gullies of Kahoolawe.

The accommodation of the leaves to air, the air
 to leaves. No, this
is not my place, but I look at it, the red cast
 over the agitated water, while
  underbranches of kiawe spin toward the light,
something braided
 in their growth, subtle musculature, rust

of age. You see it in old men on stone walls, women
 standing in line
at the market or curb. Some well of liquid, gloss
 of suppurated flesh, vanished, dropped off
  the cliff of being, and like filaments exposed,
these bulbs broken,
 these ashen reminiscences of light.

What was it flittering above the waves at sunset,
 ruddy turnstone
or black noddy? I put my body in the chop
 and rocked with it briefly. Island on which
  thought laps day and night. Arms of beach heliotrope,
rhythm to pull
 with and against. Wave passing through the sea

dispersing energy and gill. My dreams are thick here,
	truckloads of brick
backed up over a cliff, the blue monotony
	of afternoon television music
		two apartments to the south with children's voices
breaking on the
	rocks. We can stand only so much lanai.

The clouds begin to look like clouds everywhere. The boat
	dragging the rim
of the visible world past has taken the world
	with it. Nothing comes to the broken grass,
		and now, not just the one, but the other, mother
as well as father,
	lift their transmuted voices sleepily

over the oceans, wondering how it came to be
	so long so fast.
And the boy tagging along behind the three girls
	shouts, "Wait for me," which they do, and Dennis,
		whom I barely know, starts walking along the coast,
and here and there
	stops to look at things, the world of things, this.

Savage Baggage (2001)

FIRST WAKING

I wake, and it is dark. This is the first
waking. I wake, and it is still dark. This
is the second. There is a third, sometimes.
Sometimes a fourth. Each time I am dreaming.
Thick blankets thrown over old furniture.
Whose house is this? We have met here before,

I think, though we were different people.
Sometimes I do not know where I am going,
except into the next room. Sometimes I do.
Sometimes it seems like the first waking.
I am with someone who always moves away,
who urges me on by disappearing.

GRABBING FLIES

Dearest D., when I first came here, I thought
what savage baggage, what glossy tongs.
A gulag with a greeter, things to buy.
The wind fills up the day. Grass glistens.
The thread by which the button hangs is fine,
though I'm not sure the smile I wear is mine.

You see what I'm reduced to. Grabbing flies
out of the air, this scimitar of wings
flittering, need preceding everything.
I veer at the fleeing dragonflies
and gnats. I veer to keep myself aloft,
as though the air were fire, movement water.

SUN, RAIN, MOON, PAIN

The end approaches. Tomorrow I'm sent back
to the small clenchings in the gut, the smiles,
the garden full of bugs, the heat, the pull
and haul of things, the never knowing if,
the world we thought we made (and probably did),
the sun, the rain, the moon, the pain. Oh D.,

If you have ever had a thought for me,
have it again. Much rather would I,
though it cost me half my hair, stay out here
where the fox bites the rabbit through the neck
and doesn't call it love. One short, high shriek
and it's all over. Air so clean it squeaks.

BIRTH

A clenched roar. Low, hard. Is there a word
for what came through the briefly swung door, came
and went, nineteen years ago? It comes and goes
still, and it says, though it says nothing, here
is the hard thing you want to know and don't.
The wave comes in from China quietly

enough. The stars move slowly in their grooves.
But what do they know, who only live
forever? Or since they don't, maybe they, too,
scream as they fall, out where there is no end
to falling. And isn't that a tiny groan
the wave makes, throwing itself on the sand?

WHOLE WAY DOWN

How can I write of it so soon, who am
still there? The high cliff above the sea,
the dripping banyan, the simple pews.
Nowhere is not more far away than this.
I almost threw a stone for all of us,
out over the edge, the whole way down.

I would have lost it, I suppose, or else
heard nothing when it hit. I would have thought
who were you, little stone? How far is down?
Though I need not ask. It is the moment when,
or nearly when, you sit on the stone wall
at the world's end and ask to be forgiven.

MY DOG, MY HEART

Dullness, my adequate companion, my more
than durable equal, my dog, my heart, my bone,
the waves (convenient symbols) throw themselves
ceaselessly against the rocks, as though
to start, and start again, were end enough.
OK, a paradox a day keeps thought

away. To say nothing of feeling, perception,
truth, beauty and you. Out where the eye
stops seeing, out where there's only sky to break
against, the little waves do thrash, the fish
dash silently through the seas, and the seas dash,
too. None of them has heard of me or you.

I DID

She asked me, D., to lie down with her. I did.
We had been married more or less forever.
She asked me to pretend I was sixteen.
I would evanesce if I did, I said.
She said, tell me a story, a true story.
I did. I told her there was no such thing.

She said, tell me I will not die. Tell me
my arms are beautiful. I did, I did.
Tell me the earth will keep me when you are gone.
The earth will keep you. I will not go.
I will, of course, but I told her otherwise.
Truth lasts only a day, beauty a month.

ALL THE WAY TO THE CEILING

I'm sitting in a room. The light is mixed.
I'm sitting here, sitting, when suddenly
I don't know why. And why I don't know why.
Is it true, D., we spend our lives this way,
sitting in a room somewhere, wondering?
What a powerful thing a room must be.

A thing for going into and out of.
It was a room, I'm told, I came to first,
as it will be, undoubtedly, at last.
The walls go all the way to the ceiling here,
one wedged tight with everything ever thought,
the other plaster. Dust made useful, upright.

A DECENT HAPPINESS

Old friend, thin fissure of the brain, small sip
of water, you and I, it seems, are meant
for weather, the condition of the cloud
passing. The sky at this hour glistens,
as if a decent happiness were real,
the birds weren't fragments of a first idea.

I want to know, D., what a cloud says.
What the last afternoon in March means.
Where silence goes. What these words break down.
If grass this green in January seems
equal to bananas in Toledo.
Who killed Cock Robin. What his weapon was.

SOMETHING WITHOUT NAME

Long toiling over rope. Tapes. Sequences
of blue. Months embalming swamp.
Sun fills the leaves the way light bloats a bulb.
Clustered at the window, jiggled by wind.
Spring. Brush cut back along the meadow's edge.

Take three silences and lay them out
like skinned animals on the floor. Nothing
is as it was. Out from behind the door,
a slow look. Wind panthers down the grass.
Trout lilies breach across the darkened path.

Light creeps toward us over the blackened lake.
I thought of you, D., what I am to do,
now that the past is past. I write you from
a greater distance. Have thicker things
to say, less time. More something without name.

"The One Good Bite in the Saw Grass Plant" (2002)

A FLIGHT OF WILLETS

The way a flight of willets picks itself up
like a sack of loose fluttering feathered sticks
and slides across the shorebreak without
ever getting more than a foot off the ground
and keeps deciding, but always changing its mind,
where to land next, and you keep thinking,
now it will land, now it will make up its mind,
since it's clear that it has one, all ninety
or a hundred together, thinking the same
watery thought that seems always about
to be runneling off but never does, a thought
it keeps having but reinventing,
carried always onto the next stretch of beach
where the crabs are fat and apparently reckless,
everyone talking and eating at the same time,
and time beginning to tick in the bones
when all of them lift higher and higher, and look,
they're gone. Again.

SEEING THE FLORIDA PANTHER

It was moonless the night I saw one.
It was cloudless and starless, too.
I drove down to the end of the road,
where the road truly ends, a snaggle
of improbable rhizomes, and stood
in the cloudless starless moonless dark,
trying to breathe without breathing,
listening to every wrinkle in the air,
every bug exhale, every snake sniff.
Once, I remember, a plane passed over,
high, so high I could barely hear it.
At first I thought it might be a star
scratching a small slit in the dark.
I crouched low to the ground.
Like a rabbit in a wolf's gaze, I froze.
Nothing could see me, I thought.
They would never know I had been here,
whoever they were. I was glad
for the moonless light, glad
for my dull sand-colored coat,
my cloudless omnivorous eyes,
though I was a long way off
and beginning to disappear.
If I do, look for my shadow.
It's folded into the saw palmetto.

I COME TOO CLOSE

It knows when, the great white heron,
I come too close. Though I don't know what
it thinks I want. It would be nice
if it took my watching it
as simple praise. I do not want
the raw little racer it caught for lunch.
My diet calls for things that move
hardly at all. I would not touch
its chick, if it had one, or flash
a camera in its face. Agreed,
the space between us can't be crossed,
though when I try to narrow it
an inch or two, as now, I catch
something in the way it packs
its apparatus in a bag—
beak, legs and wings—and flaps off squawking,
annoyed, it would seem, with little man.
Who runs himself around,
but can't get off the ground.

SKIMMERS: A DISTRACTION DISPLAY

I love the skimmers, though this is not about them.
I love their long heavy split-level bill.
I even love the term "lower mandible,"
which sounds like a country on the far side
of Tibet, where the last snow leopard is trying
not to be seen, which also is not what this is about.
The bill is so heavy that when they rest, they turn
their heads and lay it across their backs, or,
just drop the front end of it in the sand at their feet.
This is not about that, as I said, but to see them
slice the body of the ocean open in one stroke,
an operation from which the ocean always recovers,
is almost enough to keep me from having to mention
this, which is finally what this is about. The world
coming apart.

RAIN IN THE SWAMP

Something like wind woke me. It was still dark.
I lay there listening to it gather strength,
slowly at first, then rapidly and hard.
The rain is filling up the swamp, I said,
the shallow alligator holes, the scorched
patches of saw-grass prairie, pinnacle
that lies like broken coral on a beach.
It's not just fish that live in water. Things
that came ashore often go back, or live
where land and water come to some rough agreements.
Something in all of us wants to go back.
To a muddy bank, say. Or disappear
into some thick rushes for a day or two.
If I could, I would spend the day banking
and skimming over the tops of the mangroves
with the kites, scooping up air by the wingful,
scattering it like seed in a furrow.
Who thought that being human was enough?
Or, that it was different from the plunge
head first into a river for a fish.

I GO OUT INTO THE BAY IN A KAYAK

at low tide. There might be an inch between me
and the peninsula's marly run-off.
I couldn't be any closer to the earth
if I tried, here where it is land one hour
and sea the next. Birds blow by in clouds,
driven by the fronts. I don't know what they are,
they move so fast. They must need rest.
But there go the wings like flashing knives,
and the shadow they drag across the water.
What sort of a feast it is, or will be,
I'm not told, but I know when I've been invited.

from MARL

10
Today I walked down the trail
between pine island and the saw-grass prairie.

Off to the right,
saw-grass as far as I could see.

I wanted to be out in that place somehow,
surrounded by it, disappeared into it.

I put myself there the only way I could,
walked for half a day out into it,

and when I was far enough away,
I sat down in the muck.

The saw-grass waved above my head,
its bayonets clattering in the wind.

A small cloud went by,
chased by a few birds.

I sat there a long time, trying not to think,
trying to unbe and be at the same time.

After a while, a long while,
I grabbed the marl with both hands and squeezed.

And, yes, I rubbed some of the ooze,
that pasty gray clay, on my cheeks and forehead.

I pulled up a stalk of saw-grass
and bit the one good bite there is in the saw-grass plant,

the one at the base where the leaves are all together briefly
before they shoot up, tough, toothed and separate, into the world,

and with the serrated blade of one of its leaves,
cut my thumb.

I let it bleed a little,
then washed it in the slough.

Delicate Bait (2003)

AUNT EL

She was said to have never bathed.
And to have stacked the rooms
of her house with newspapers.
I don't even know whose aunt she was.
Maybe nobody's aunt. Aunt Blank.
Though the glee in mother's eyes,
as she hands me the keys to this
damp closet, tells me, of course, what else.

I see her rattling about with a wagon
or bag, draped in a straggling dress
and bonnet, asking at back doors, cringing
under the stares of housegirls and cooks.
She couldn't have done it alone,
on her subscription, presuming she had one.
Presuming, too, she could read.
Maybe she needed to fill a room
in a hurry, to admire her handiwork,
to say, this is my room full of words.
She would say this to no one, of course,
thinking that no one would ever know.
There she is in a robe, tattered. She holds
the lantern away from her body,
as though she were paper herself.

There were farms somewhere
in back of my family, a barn
in back of my grandparents' house.
The people who live there now know nothing

about us, don't see the spot of blood
on the driveway, the ambulance idling
at the side door, don't see Aunt El
or her baffled eyes, going her rounds
in a stinking skirt, talking to dogs,
scattering children like flies. Even
the chickens avoided her mournful cluck.

Nor do they see the mayor of Avalon,
or the priest who lived with his sister,
the unmarried schoolteacher, the man
who ran out on his wife, or the one
who stole. They don't see the man
who killed himself drinking or the woman,
his wife, he left with the children,
or the chauffered limousine with someone,
concealed, in back. And certainly
they don't see Bertha, dead on the floor
of her unheated house in Camden.

I come from somewhere I've never been,
or somewhere I've been but don't remember.
I need to know that I've been where I've been
and lived there and loved what there was to love.
If I could, I would choose this woman, this aunt
whom no one mentioned (and no one forgot),
to take me there. She teaches me how to knock
at a back door, how to ask the smallest question.

LISTENING

I can still hear Robert Frost. He was the first.
Who struggled up to the front, his white hair tossed
across his eyes. The undergraduates grinned
to hear a man snap twigs among the scholars.
I remember Auden, too, in the great hall
at Balliol, telling us he was sick.
He had come home to die, and he was sick,
he said, of "the whole fucking lot" of us.
He read for an hour without books or notes.
I can't remember what he read that night,
November in Chicago, but Lowell bowed
and thanked us at the end, a man half dragged
ashore, a fish thrashed out of water.
Basil Bunting, in London, reading *Briggflatts*
in his chopped Northumbrian brogue.
Kinnell stood up in Milwaukee once
and said, before his own, the hard poem
called "Hard Rock" by the poet, Etheridge Knight.
And here in Bloomington, Hugo, holding
the crab at bay. In two months, he had lost
a lung. In two years, died. He, too, recited,
hands palms down on the stone slab in front of him.
And Olson. I sat in the chapel pew
at Beloit, the songs across my lap,
and watched his poems jackknife across the page.
John Berryman in Madison, jerking
his Henry on a stick, Merrill whispering
into his book, the look of a thinking

monkey on his face. Vohznesensky
nailed his Russian poems to the floor.
Ginsberg with finger cymbals, Rothenberg
with gourds. Duncan conducted, unfolding poems
in the air, birds of a single wing.
Leather-jacketed Ted Hughes, resonant
and stolid, stood with one hand hidden.
Empson at Oxford, a squeaking reed.
MacDiarmid in full main at Edinburgh.
Kizer in Manchester. The pale MacNeice.
And Kunitz at the embassy in Warsaw.
Where, to six or seven, he read his poem
on having his pocket picked in Rome. But more,
he read the one I read his whole work twice to find.

In Paterson I tried to buy that poem
in a store. They thought it was a joke.
I read Venetian history for a year,
only to have Pound die before I got there.
I had our conversations all worked out.
He would read me the thirteenth canto,
and I would come back with that song from Lawes.
He would say something, then, I don't know what,
and the long slide of history would stop
long enough to blur before our consciousness.
We would see it, though, a swipe across the sky,
and say "There it is" or "There it is, there,"
before the call to dinner or the nurse
with medicines took everything away.

I don't know what I thought that day, if it was
a day, and not a year or mere flash of sunlight
off the gray river in the afternoon
or taint of bookdust at the Grolier,
but I remember hearing words I knew,
or thought I knew, handled like rough stone,
sharpened like a stick.

I read a poem in a book then, too,
put it down, forgot it, went on living.
And somewhere, later, when I wasn't looking,
the light changed suddenly or the thing
I thought I was got up and walked away.

TRUTH OF THE MATTER

for Bridget

I remember the dreamy deer in the park at Oxford
grazing under the evenly cropped trees.
The leaves came down from the sky and stopped
just above the heads of the placid deer,
who, when they cared, poured like muscled water
through the trunks, appearing and disappearing
among them, herding together, their stick little legs
breaking the silence barely among the leaves
which, as I said, all came down in a line like a shade.

The day I came to watch from behind the fence
the innocent gray deer prink in their perfect park,
away from the traffic on High Street, away, too,
from the great names of the dead, the ghosts
of the living, agog, moving among them, touching
the stones, saying the strange names aloud
in a twisted tongue, phrases mastered at breakfast,
standing, rapt, where the martyr stood alone
or running a finger down the spine of a book.

On that day, tired of the fixed stare of the great
greatness, from which we had only partly come,
from which we had barely come at all, in fact,
watching the frail deer, posing themselves beneath the oaks,
which all came down like thick lava and stopped,
stuck in the air, I knew when the dog had come.

I did not see it at first, and was not sure
what it was, when the men ran panting past,
waving their arms, and the deer flashed in
and out of the shadows, sinewy and pert, turning
and leaping in unison, a real corps de ballet.

One of them died that day and the dog was caught
and, somewhere out of the way, killed.
I remember it loping out of the woods,
slavering its bloody jaws, cornered at last.
It stood while the wheezing men undid its collar.
And my youngest daughter, three at the time,
who understood nothing, from whom I tried,
wrongly perhaps, to keep the truth of the matter, cried.

WHY WE'RE HERE

Before we can properly excuse ourselves,
I am sitting in the shade under the oak tree
talking about farming with the old man,
and my wife is out among the flowers
with his wife. I know nothing about farming,
but the words fall effortlessly from my mouth.
My wife comes back holding an iris clipping,
and they join us in the shade with the flies.
We are suddenly members of the family,
rocking and swatting. We talk about things
as though we had waited all winter long
for the snow to melt. A bluebird
flies into the box on the fencepost
as we talk, and a rabbit hops lethargically
across the driveway down by the car
where I left the mower I brought
to be sharpened. That's why we're here.

He is the last man in the county
who can sharpen a push mower.
And he is not easy to find. And,
he takes his time. We have found him, though,
and he is taking most of the afternoon
to tell us he thinks he can do it
and for how much. We shake on it.

I am getting my mower sharpened
by first having my flaked faith in the ways of people
touched up and my disinclination to old age
abated. It is costing me eight dollars.

CLEARING IN THE WEST

for my father, dying

In the midst of being awake on a Tuesday.
Walking the heartless corridor in the heat,
head petrified with memo and deadline.
Pacing the edges of a way of doing things
I once knew the need of, he now responding
with his eyes only. You say something
to him and he closes them. Or moves them off
in the direction of the innocuous curtain.
What use is speech? What are we doing here,
and why are there these thousand miles?
I read a fistful of poems in a taxi,
and maybe this is the moment, humidity
ninety per cent, leaves gasping for breath,
a thankless thin blue to the sky and all
these fresh frightened faces clustered
around the bed asking for their turn. Move over,
they say. I get to carry the pole now.
I get to paddle in back. It's clearing, he'd say,
clearing in the west. And so we rode
on hope and the bad road for another
thousand afternoons. Now the west is here.
The wide awful brim of a tired hat.
May the way be clear, the way west.
May the clouds part and you, the hard blue sky,
bend a little, bend down and take this bag
of hope who loved nothing more than your blueness.
Whether you showed it to him or not.

THE TABLE

As in a Bonnard,
or maybe just
the Bonnard on this post card,
the woman sitting at the table
seems to be part of the table.
Places are set for two others,
but they seem to be late,
or can't come, or fell down,
or decided it was too
lovely a day to sit
in front of a brown door
fingering the few cherries
left in the basket, eating
another roll, a second peach.
Besides, the woman is hardly there.
Her face is turned away,
her attention fixed
on something her hands
are doing in a bowl.
Her voice barely rises
above a mumble. Hair
falls down the side of her head
as though it didn't matter
that eighty or so years later
we would be walking
along a coastline in the rain,
having once again, and elsewhere,

found the soul's own
flickering habitation, aghast
at the drenched way
the feathers clung
to the bones of the dead gannet
tossed among
the gannet-colored stones.
The wind whiffled its way
down the coast, looking
for something likely,
a feather, a blade of grass,
a finger, whatever
is made of wind or has
the lift and surge
of its idlest inclinations
knitted to its wrist.
The clouds moved off
mumbling to themselves,
with places
already set for us.

THE WAY TWO HORSES STAND

The way two horses stand next to one another in a field,
and we are coming into the village in a car to have lunch
with old friends at the deli, and the sun and the wind
are helping one another slowly up a difficult stairway.

The way the fox crossing the field lowers its head and squints
as though swimming underwater through a stream of bugs,
the kind that only that morning found there was a world
and have only till evening to solve the mysterious silence.

The way the eastern phoebe in the nest above the door holds
fiercely to the hatching of her five white eggs, round as peas,
and though we come and go, wondering whether it matters
if stars collide, guarding its muddy purchase on the possible.

The way the clouds amble along whispering among themselves.
The way, the daily way, we have of deciphering what they're saying.
The way sky darkens before rain, and the rain hesitantly
steps down into the grass, as though into freshly drawn bathwater.

DELICATE BAIT

The shell of the meal broken
and sucked clean, the ocean
chewing up the beach beyond the palms
made it seem that eating a simple meal
there by the ocean at night
on an island heaved up millennia ago
in fiery explosions, and the fish
having leapt out of the same water,
bodies of a movement of that sea,
ocean larger than anything
on earth, would suffice. That we should come
and go, eating the few thousand meals,
a few hundred fish, a room full of grains,
that we should put the world in our mouths
and swallow, become the fish,
the deer, the goat, the field of wheat,
walking graveyard with no stones, body of death
and the world. Out of the fish
and our sitting there, out of our
being together briefly in that place,
our scattered and gathered trying-to-be,
one to the other, less evanescent,
less brief and accidental, something,
so that when, in the impending hour,
oblivious, hour of cancellation and woe,
we turned back to our lives, whatever they were,
we would have, or keep, maybe a phrase,

a sense of the light, the look
of the fish arranged on its bier of rice,
the voice of the ocean, continuous, around us,
the burning of that hour together, something,
something even memory cannot reach,
wave that comes across an ocean,
only to fall gratefully onto the sand.

On the north side of the island,
region of small icons and cairns,
in the voice of that place, tumble
of rock back into the sea from which it came,
people stack one rock on another,
two or three, a cluster,
sometimes a single rock set out alone
on the edge of that other rock,
the island itself, saying here,
a flame in a red dress, I was here, and the fish
is a part of my body, and I thank
the fish and the cook and the person
who brought it to me and those
at the other tables making cairns
out of words and gestures,
glances in every direction.
It was beginning to slide, wash
back into the silence from which it came.
It was happening to me, to us,

and I was watching it, lifted
one fork at a time into my mouth,
into the mouths of the others, those
I was with, those I was almost with,
those gone and going before,
those for whom I am the one going before,
scattering, as when alarmed,
not scattering really, but moving just beyond
the ends of our fingers,
when, swimming among them,
we reach out to touch them,
almost become one ourselves,
fish in the sea.
And, that more delicate bait,
the you and the me.

THE PLACE WE CAME ASHORE

The small colony of black noddies
tucked up into its cave. The way
every time we go there, little spurts
of clouddust or shoremist spatter us
and on each of the narrow ledges up under
the glowering volcanic cap birdlime streaks
downward in a floral exuberance.
The sea comes heaving in on time, every time,
and the birds flap out now and again just
over the top of it. Try as hard as we can
to prevent it, they disappear into the light,
shredding itself to pieces on the sea's back.
I don't know why when I think of it, I think
this is the place love found us, away
almost from our own nature, looking back
up into the land as though from another world.
As though this was the place we came ashore
all those thousands of years ago, looking
for what we would learn to call each other.

Half/Mask (2007)

FIRST MASK

Take that smooth rock,
the one out there
next to the sky,
for the middle of the forehead.
Something drifts around the mouth.
The lips go fleshy on one side
and blubber off. Thought slides through
like the tatter of a cloud.
The feather needs oiling, or replacing,
I can't tell which.
In the neighborhood of the brain,
a small smoothed fragment
of the day, rock like space.
The ear, though, should go
where the nose is, the nose
off to one side
hunting for oranges
and gossip. The smile, it
should be bigger, stupid even.
You can look like that
and still eat. You can fish
and go to the moon
on the same hook.
Part of it needs to be wood,
though bone is around.
Bits of colored glass
and an eyeball made of tar.

Tar may be hard,
so let it be chicken wire,
bluebird, a smear
of misunderstanding and dirt,
some plain scratches.
To show pleasure.
Or pain. Either one.

THE STONES AT CALLINISH,
ISLE OF LEWIS

A boarded-up hotel beside
a fishing pier, a pub. Above them both,
a church crouched on a hill. Whoever brought
Christ to this desolate coast did it
with sword and fire, and it's not clear today
whether it took, or whether the slow seep
of centuries, the long winter nights,
would ever let anything be that wasn't
as sullen as the hill. The village
is that way, too. When you step outside,
there it is, the universe, all of it,
the glare of it pure, God's unshaven face
so close your skin rasps. Whoever raised
these stones did a good job of vanishing, too,
though the longer I stand here, the more
it seems it was deeper into the genes
they went, not just into the air.

WHITE WINGED SWARMING

1
Sunday.
Only a few crows this morning.
A treeful of starlings
down by the road.
I walk up past
a hill of old tires
and out onto
the rolling plateaus
of sandy waste,
thinking of those
who left their ships
locked in ice
and set out across
continents of snow
with a single thought,
who ate their dogs,
one by one, who pulled
the sled themselves.
And of the ones
who found them, the tiny
separated teeth,
tins of perfectly
preserved pears.
Across a small ravine,
a scree of stoves,
torn bags, things

I can't make out,
the usual stuff.
At home, for hours,
I look for the hint
of dead animal,
rotted fruit.
I lift my sleeve
to my face
several times,
hugging it to me.

2
I'm up on the dump again,
looking at things.
This isn't a Romantic dump
or a Classical one.
It's the dump at the edge
of town, the one where the road
flashes on the other side
of a few spindly trees
and the cars go by
and don't stop.
It's the one where they took
the old rug from the basement
and the box full of jars
saved for a life

you were sure
you were going to live.
Your radio with the bent
aerial and the dust
is up there, too,
and the stuff
you couldn't do without
all those years.
It's up there,
buried in a shallow grave.
Two gulls tear
at a chicken wing.
A third one screams.
I pull at a piece
of old plastic bag.
I pull and pull,
but I don't come
to the end of it.
It rips open the wound
in the ground
and shows me . . . well,
you know what it shows me.
We were both there
when it happened,
when the earth started
spitting us back.

3

It's a good place to study
the behavior of certain birds.
And if you look hard,
you can see the world up there,
the heap we make
with our caring and not caring.
It's all there,
crows thrown over it
like crumbs of a burnt cake.
The gulls scream something
I can't make out.
When I move closer,
when I try to get
right up into their feather
and flap, when I try to keep
this blackened bit
of banana to myself,
tossing it back
to the back of my throat,
gnashing it down
at a gulp, they hop away.
Not far,
just to the next
scratched-over place in the sand,
where, sleepy but alert,
they wait for the next
spasm of need,
truckload of plastic,
crushed grease.

4

And I go into the store
and I think, here
is where it starts.
I handle the little item
in its smooth plastic bubble.
I rub the bubble,
soft as a newborn skull.
I know a crow
who wants to pick through
these glazed arrangements
of salt. I know a gull
who sits on a lamp post
waiting. And here I am
scavenging the aisles,
looking for something prenatal,
wrapped in my own bubble.

5

I knew it would happen.
Not where or how or when,
but I knew it would.
I didn't know it,
but I knew it.
It's hard to explain.

Something would break.
You know,
some little thing.
And there it would be,
broken forever.

And I would give my life to it.
I would not understand it,
and I would have
no name for it.
But I would give
everything to it.
Not knowing it
at first, but doing it.

There was no other way.
There was to have been
no other way.

Everything
and the giving
of everything
to it.

6
How I love these gulls,
even the stealing
from one another.
They have left
their old home, the sea,
to follow the veins
of garbage, inland.
Up there on the hill,
the bulldozer
backs and fills
under a cloud of them.
I call it a cloud.

It's more like a
scrambling flutter.
Above that,
up where the true clouds are,
a strange wheeling, slow.
A gathering, perhaps,
before a departure.
A whispering, out of range,
about the old ways,
about the new.
I stand and watch it,
longing to go,
longing to be gone.

7
Which gull is it
that never sees
the land? Have I
imagined it,
out there riding
the swells or hung
on a long hook
of wind? The world
of the gull is nearly
the world itself,
but this gull sits
on a solitary hump
of sea, a rolling
shrug of the universe,

and waits. This gull
mates forever.
To wind, water,
sun, and rain.
To the one gull
that finds her.
They make a nest
of themselves
in the curve
between two waves.
And their mating,
no one has seen.
It is done aloft,
at night, and may take
years. Years
circling in the dark,
wingtip
brushing wingtip.
The young ride
on their mother's back
until they can fly,
and then leave.
The father
has left already.
And the mother.
She is the last,
but she leaves, too.
It is not known
if the young survive,
or whether perhaps

these are the kind
who leave their species,
who live where nothing
is fixed, where stillness
glides over great deeps.
We have to rely
on the odd sighting,
people, boatbound
and lonely, who,
in a world shrunk
to the world itself,
need to believe
they have been there,
that being there
is being itself.

8
The highway holds the curve
of the river close.
A land form rises to the right,
skims along a flank
of glacial frieze, and there,
halfway up, a white,
winged swarming. By now,
I know the signs, raw scrape
in the ground, relentless gulls.
Too far into this scheme
of feeding, of having to be
someone, of having to think

my way toward morning,
of reaching the day's end
somewhere I wasn't at dawn,
dragged by a harsh, migratory
urge across a rake of clean,
hard, unforgiving ideas,
I give it my birdy,
sideways eye, and drive on.

DRIVING NORTH THROUGH THE MIDDLE OF THE CONTINENT IN LATE FALL LOOKING FOR SNOW

There, at last, the first small tatters of torn cloth scattered
    in the shorn fields,
fields folded into themselves, fields outlined in stripped
    trumpet vine, black weed, muck of the sort hawks
        sit above for hours. The fragment of stained shroud
held between two
    pieces of glass in a glass case, freed now

of the body. But on into the dusk, the headlights
    spreading under
a sky, wide, descending, brooding over the day's
    long hours. Then, on low banks, even the fat
        lips of ditches, those facing north, a drape, as at
some spread feast, page
    in a book on which nothing is printed,

or, under small clusters of young trees stunned into one
    posture for months,
a cloth, wrapping, anything quick to ornament
    bleakness or make the eventual seem
        accompanied and thick, full of the thing it was.
Night lays calmness
    aside, and the first sputtering crackles

of white fire pop out of the air, rushing the headlights,
    the plunge forward
into the cataract dark, wind thickening speech.
    Swaddled in the hours, we stare down a white
        tunnel of thought, and when daylight leaks back, the trees
float out to us,
    freed now from fields no longer theirs, or there.

UTITSIALANGAVIK

It is not clear whether that is sea
in the background, but I am sure
that in the foreground a group of small stones
gathers around a large upstanding one.
They look like a hungry audience,
anxious to know what the tunillarvik,
for that is the name of the upstanding stone,
has to say. They lean forward,
waiting patiently for word.
The tunillarvik has the markings
of deepest veneration (tunillarvik means
"object of veneration") streaked downward
over its smooth pate. Long strings
of lime-white bird droppings.
For untold eons, gulls have sought this place
as brief refuge from the daily squabble over food
or as perch from which to view
the incremental movement of the hours.
The least and most migratory
of Arctic forms brought together.

Around about, and as far as we can see,
forever, an inhospitable beauty.

"In the old days, we lived on the land.
We carefully followed in the footsteps
of our ancestors. Ever traveling,

we killed every living thing we and our dogs could eat.
Such was our necessity,
living the only life we knew."

The little congregation of the stones
with its white-haired leader ponders its next move,
perhaps along the utitsialangavik
("the pathway one must follow"),
perhaps not.

HALF MASK

Maybe it's the half that's there,
the mask itself,
left face or right.

Or, since the wearer,
the carver and wearer,
the painter, is now gone,

it is he or she
who, in being gone,
plays the part

of being both here
and there at the same time,
in and out of the world,

above and below,
half what he is,
half what he wants to be,

walking along a path,
but chatting with the dead
about the snow

beginning to fall at dusk
and the light coming on
in the house across the field.

The dead reassure him.
The dying, too.
He would be lost without them.

The snow comes down
in a way he spends
most of the morning

trying to find words for,
words that would keep it
falling somewhere always.

But the snow keeps falling,
and the carver tires.
Eating and lying down

are part of the thing
he has in mind.
So he leaves the mask unfinished.

WHEN THE STONES REVOLTED

Nothing I know wants nothing, even stones.
I've seen them lying in the riverbed,
exhausted, toward the end of summer,
and the river has thinned down to a film
of pure transparency, when the stones
revolted and rose against the river banks,
which moved against them with such rootedness
and loamy weight, they fell back shouting
to the stars from which they'd come, don't leave us.
Which the stars heard, but only faintly,
and when they shone next, poured down on them
a trickle of something the stones almost
remembered. Though it was a long way off,
and the air was hazy, so they said nothing.

LAST SUMMER OF THE CENTURY

Cromwell was married in the church next door.
Hard to imagine Cromwell a husband.
Milton is buried there, Frobisher as well.
A hundred feet to the east, a small plaque
where the first bombs fell in 1940.
Gap-toothed fragments of the old city wall
now split new glass high rises with see-through
external elevators. For six weeks,
we took a class as though on a long walk
across a meadow toward a waiting barge.
A flowered barge, with curlicues and ice.
We were to float downriver, not too fast,
and then I suppose into the North Sea
through the mines the Germans put there,
still clutched underwater to their rusting chains.
It was not like that, of course. It was one
brilliant day after another. And then,
a slow surfacing to muffle the kind
of bends you get from coming home fast.
Too fast. From too far away. To a yard
overgrown with weeds, heat like permanent
migraine, windless nights, dirt turned to stone.

We liked the wine bar on the "podium,"
as they called the platform that ran between
the blocks and towers, hairdresser, theatre,
the church with its famous dead, the squared pond.

Very modern. Very 1970.
We sat outside, sipped wine in the sunshine.
When there was sunshine. The barge had a leak,
of course, persistent, and the meadow tilted.
Toward Smithfield Market and the All Bar One.
Men in bloody aprons taking tea break
as the dark-suited masses rushed to work.
It was OK, though. More than OK,
it was Jack London in the morning,
disappearing into "the Abyss,"
Fortnum and Mason's in the afternoon.
What Pound called "the sturdy unkillable
infants of the very poor," dying in fact
before they were thirty, followed by
jars of the greengage plum for Mom, clinging
at eighty-eight to the ledge of her life
above Cherry Creek Parkway and the spare
white mountaintops that ply the western sky.
The creek itself is dry. Has been for years.

It was not easy walking in the city,
but you aren't in London if you don't walk.
We hiked south out of Piccadilly Circus
past a gaggle of international banks,
through dazed bands of day-trippers from small towns
in the Vosges, villages on the upper
Danube, suburbs of Kyoto, Sydney,
Atlanta. Into Waterloo Place, where
heroic posing over the Crimea
clashed with the Gap on Regent Street. Much as

extremities of *The Waste Land* mangled
the need to be in Paris for the weekend.
Wide steps cascaded past the ICA,
into the park Clarissa crosses
in the opening movements of her book.
We would look in vain for the pelicans
we'd seen in the first minutes of the film,
or "sandwich men shuffling and swinging."
On down past the Horse Guards Parade,
the likeness of Viscount Mountbatten
guarding the sandbagged outlet to Downing Street
(terror of the IRA), into the bunker
of another unfinished war, also sandbagged,
under the Foreign Office with its prime
ministerial bed still made, the blundering
and luck palpable in the tight spaces,
recorded wail of the air raid siren,
Churchill addressing still a hushed nation
through its well-mannered proceeding under
the seething rain of fire. Somewhere near
the high held gaze of Florence Nightingale
and the blank-eyed stare of the generic
grieving woman of imperial war,
up under some branches, among car horns,
in the froth of thinking, we came upon
the black glistening statue of Sir John
Franklin. At his feet, on either side
of the pediment, lists of the doomed crews
of the *Erebus* and *Terror.* Who perished
so utterly far from anything displayed

in a park or a shop window, anyone
dying in a doorway of starvation
or bomb dropped in the front garden, one
of whom stood that last summer on the shore
of Queen Maud Gulf perhaps, alone, or with
the two or three of his mates still alive,
glimpsed over a ridge by a native hunter,
but not approached, the shade of whom was found
in a later century and lifted
out of a silence he might have cherished,
watching a few guillemots ruck past,
puffins crash into stony water,
the long horizon and low pebbly beach,
an almost featureless version of the world,
sun like a thin chemise over the cold,
come to seem the anteroom to heaven.

We wound our way up Long Acre, through
the Seven Dials, looking for a cheese store,
one we'd stumbled into the week before.
We forgot it was back among the porn shops
and massage parlors in Soho. And so,
kept walking in the hot afternoon light
in the last summer of the century
toward Ludgate, no longer a circus, and a pint
at The Olde Bell in back of St. Bride's
where, among the shadows and the murmurs,
a man read a novel at the bar.

New Poems (2008)

CARRIED ACROSS A FIELD

I say these things so they will not be forgot.
Anything, a shoe, even these thoughts, can be dropped
by the side of the road and left there. Or picked up
and carried across a field or mountaintop.

Hands that have lost touch. The way cloud
comes into the sky as though out of a fold
in thought. See the way wood has chosen
grass to imitate, grass that has woven

itself to water. Picked up on the way
from one life to another, you couldn't say
why exactly. Though it mattered then to slow down,
to pick something up that was on the ground.

POEMS I MIGHT HAVE WRITTEN

The one that made no mention of the self,
except to say she'd always looked at rocks
wherever she went, turning them over
with her foot, scumbling among them for a streak
of fire, a flake of the creation's first
gray knowledge of itself, who broke open
geodes like a safe, hoping to find
a hint of extinction's whereabouts.
The one about the way the people left
the city when the lights went dark, the way
the city stood there in its own shadow
and watched. The people had nowhere to go,
but they went anyway, in streams, in long
ropey flowages over the darkened bridges.

BENEATH A CLOUD

So much of it is or seems (who knows the difference?)
transplanted, uprooted, dangling, frittered.
I like invisible, though visible
has its properties, proprieties, its strange
amazements. I'm equal to the bees, let's say,
transparent, bespattered, rearranged, though not
without being first arranged. How or by what,
I don't ask. Gathered, scattered, secret. Here
for a moment. In terrible, terrifying,
ordinary distance from matter and things,
from reasons I can't see the reason for.
Lucid and fluid, I look out the window.
Do things in stages, leave them unfinished,
believing that nothing ever becomes
completely. Is always coming about, around.
Sometimes remembered. Remembered again,
but fragmentarily, or by someone else.
Ancient, delirious, wise, unable.
Shouted across a field. Fallow, hollow,
hallowed. Done in the dark, all of it. At dawn,
on a Tuesday or Friday. All of it
always arriving. Convinced, confused. Knowing
and unknowing. A cloud beneath a cloud.
A sky bringing all of itself along.

BETWEEN MOUNTAINS

I had in good degree learned to be content with a plain way of living.
—John Woolman

Just yesterday, I was halfway up a ladder
painting a wall a devotee of stark
German Expressionism would have loved.
It was the color of dead putty, bones.
Before that, I was driving in the rain.
Across country, you could say. Ohio anyway.
Then Colorado. Along the Purgatoire,
thin river wandering through dust and scrub.
A place so far away from anything
I knew, I thought at last I'd found home.
This abandoned shack would do, I thought.
This rusted trowel. We could fix it up
and start counting whatever desert monks
keep track of, grains of sand, the narrow pass
between this desolation and the next.
As for the plain way, I know it's out there,
just over the horizon, winking its bare bulbs,
like Christmas at a high plains truck stop, a fleet
of throbbing semis angled in for the night,
no snow as yet, the only water, bottled.
There was the night we spent in—where was it?
The six or seven at the bar, the warm,
low conversation we could not make out,
a stream gone back to its source underground,
the Stetsons twisted with sweat, the mangled boots,

the gruff "good nights," the going home—to what?—
an unmade bed, a candle for a light.
And we there, not sure exactly where, except
between mountains, the bed a little lumpy,
wind sniffing at the door, and out there
in the dark coyotes yipping up a catch.

HUNTERS

Out at Pine Grove at sunset looking for cranes,
    the mauled carcass
of a deer not twenty feet away. A hunter
    comes by sprouting a vivid orange cap.
        We talk briefly, like members of neighboring tribes
whose fathers fought
    long ago to a bloody standstill,

and who now seek out the company of wild animals.
    What have you got,
he asks. Cranes, I tell him. They've been passing over
    all day. When he sees the twisted torso
        in back of me, he kneels down, thinks a minute,
says, coyotes,
    two or three of them, last night about dusk.

Following the example of an ancient priest, who
    is said to have
traveled thousands of miles with no care for comfort,
    thereby attaining a state of ecstasy
        under the pure beams of the moon, Basho left home
in August
    of the first year of Jyokyo among wails

of the autumn wind, determined to become a pure
    bride of the wind,
skeleton by the side of the road, unknown

to all but the ants and the coyotes
     of that country, said to have been some species of
featherless bird
    that sings small songs of complicated kind.

STRANGE TERRAIN

The people across the street go into the house.
They go inside as though it were the natural thing
to do. He opens the door with the key, and she follows.
They are living a life, trying to live a life,
the color of moss, clatter of ankles and grass.
They have an idea about the future. The future
as a sprig of jasmine. You can see it in their dress,
in the way they approach the door. Hesitating,
languid, they don't yet know who they are,
and it hurts them to know that, to have the sense
that something is near which they can't see, and
that it might be themselves. He moves in a slumbrous
water buffalo sort of way. Smaller and tilting
to one side, she, it is clear, will be blown away,
as birds are said to be blown off course, into
a strange terrain. Strange terrains are everywhere,
to be sure, and the strangers who make them strange,
so she will not be alone. It may feel like no one
is there, or no one who knows the avenue's flow.
I have no reason for saying it, but I say it anyway:
Nothing is ever without its principle and being.
Even so simple a thing as walking up to your door
does not go unnoticed. You, for instance,
think you are walking along a street. But, no.
You are becoming the way another has often thought.
Is beginning to think. Storms of happening sleep
beneath the cambric of the hour, and the key

that rattles in your or another's hand opens doors forever
shut forever. You will not go there without
someone saying, there are fields of drenched feather.
And the man who is sure he knows, and has the key
in his hand to prove it, whispers the word, here.

COUNTING THE STAIRS

Maybe there is no world. Maybe nothing
is what the trees have been saying for years.
I remember counting the stairs. I knew
where I was always. Seventy two
meant I'd gone too far, though the tiles on the floor
were the same up there, and the water fountain.

I want to walk away from this poem
before it tells me it may not be me
writing it. These may not be, after all,
my thoughts, rather what the trees have tried
to suggest without mentioning a thing,
without even knowing they were trees.

AWAY FROM HOME

I catch myself looking at myself,
naked in a mirror, away from home,
the sun about to rise. What is this form
at almost seventy, flesh eaten by
its nights and days, fodder for the gods?

Shadow on an urn, shape stuck upright
in the ground, tousled cloud, thought rushing through
its narrow gorges. What presumption, what
abandonment, keeps it coming back,
looking for itself, convinced it's here?

FISHERMAN'S DITTY

Goodbye to the little yard full of clover and crabgrass,
the sagging carport and the neighbors. Farewell to the rabbi
who ate nothing but pizza, to splitting wood in the driveway
on a portable stump, which the neighbors watched
from the shadows in back of their kitchens as I brought
the maul down on a life that was hardly a life at all
but a series of internal negotiations over which of us
put out the most orderly, incumbent trash of the week.
It was a life I asked for and loved and never knew why
it never seemed to be mine but a wave that washed over me,
my head full of voluptuous seaweed, shipwreck and foam.
Believe me, I love to lie here singing this fisherman's ditty,
a bit of rope in my hands for practicing my knots,
mind loosened by grog, whine of the squeezebox, wheeze
of the salts cantering out onto the deck under the stars.
Beneath the tune, unmistakable and huge, the sea's heave.

GIVING A BOX OF BOOKS AWAY

Little caskets of my former dreams,
I feed you back into the Ganges
of living perceptions, extravagant
longings, that life, no matter how
scattered, buffeted, ridden by floods
of feeling and need, can't do without.
Let somebody else finish Tasso.
Let somebody else put the citadel
of Plutarch, the shield of Proust,
on the shelf above his bed to protect him
from a life without extravagant hope.
My underlinings in Freud, my shouts
in the margins of Dostoevsky, my first
edition of *Goodbye Wisconsin,* my
*Swap and Go: Home Exchanging
As a Way of Life,* as the way of my life
becomes clear and less cluttered,
I set afloat in the sleepy bulrushes
of the delta like a child I couldn't keep.
Goodbye ambition, goodbye to keeping
around what even memory lets go.
The sea greets us like a long-lost friend
while gigantic mountains of cumulo-nimbus
collapse and inflate across the sky.

VARIATIONS ON A THEME BY SEVERAL HANDS

I'm in no hurry, but I'd like to say
that I will die somewhere. Rio, maybe.
I've never been to Rio. Never died
either, quite. Rio in a taxi, say,
my shirt open in the heat, my palms sweaty,
having avoided Carnival and the crowds,
having never wanted to go to Rio,
except at the end, and only for a way
they have of steaming mussels, in wine,
which I'll hear about in Phoenix in the rain,
when I go to Phoenix for some reason
now withheld. It will be hot in Phoenix,
and, except for that particular day, dry,
and I will probably ask myself why
Phoenix, but only as rhetorical evasion,
for I will know then why. Know, in fact,
everything I need to know. And the vendors
on the street will smile and talk about the weather,
hoping I might buy some small cadeau,
not for the money it will make them, but
for the need they'll see somewhere in my face
for something to hang loosely around my neck,
a stone perhaps, a leaf, a simple bauble,
for the ride I'll take in Rio in a cab,
the driver asking me in broken English
the name of my hotel, whether I know

his uncle in Des Moines, not to worry
about the end—he's given death a ride
before—last week in fact, a man in white,
a clean white suit, quite fitting, leather pumps.
He sat where you sit, leaning slightly
to the left, his hand quivering, face blue.
Otherwise, no resemblance to you.

POEM WITH A BOY ON A BUS

I want to wake up from something like sleep,
something in which the events of sleep,
which move too fast to be seen, mingle freely
with the knowledge that I am not asleep,
and read a poem I remember reading somewhere
about a boy sleeping on a bus in Madrid,
on a bus going away from Madrid actually,
out into the Spanish countryside at night,
countryside I've never seen, filled with night,
another country I've seen little of,
and write a poem no one understands,
that moves too fast to be understood,
that thinks understanding is a color
or an aromatic soap, that understanding
may be what the grass does all summer long
or light putting itself down slowly toward the end of day.
On the far side of the mountain, someone
is writing a sentence that has neither beginning,
middle nor end. He sits by the window and lets
the sun look over his shoulder. In the words
are the meanings of the words, but he prefers
to rub them together. That way, they murmur
things they would never understand, or need to.

OLD WOMAN WITH DOG IN FIELD

Wearing a white tennis visor
and blue cottony windbreaker,
telling Ralph, Down, silly.
Be down, and (to herself) not so damnably
up in the face of every odd bird
out for a quick check on the world.
Over-friendly, she says, pulling a full
set of ivory teeth out of her smile.
What's it like in your life?
Asked by looking off at the bluff
and muttering something about winter.
Yes, I say, looks like a hill of weather
headed this way. Ralph has pinned some
beetle to the ground, continues winsome.

EXQUISITE CLOTH

I sometimes think I'm part of a larger animal,
one cell among billions, dead, alive, and still
to come, who, together, will, in time, come to know
all that can be known. Fantastic, I realize.
But it allows me to think also of what, even
at the end of human thought, when all insight,
information, opinion, advice has been assembled
in bins or vast electronic pouches, will be
withheld from us. Though we do not have to wait
for that last innocent, elusive item of human
realization to be added to the pile, to come
into the presence of this thing I can't describe.
It is here now, whatever it is, and all of us
look out the window or across the room,
take down another book from the shelf,
or get out a pad and start scribbling, hoping
that this time it will not get away, though
truly it has no way to escape, much less be,
apart from those who cannot know it, ever,
and who reach, if they're lucky, this tender
edge of being with an unforseen relief.

So, rather than wait for human intelligence
to finish its job, for someone—though who?—to say,
"We now know what can be known, go home
and weed your garden," which might not happen
for millennia, or, quite possibly, passed by

unnoticed one Saturday in Bruges as Kant—
whether or not he ever set foot in Bruges—
was admiring some exquisite cloth in a window
as his coach rolled over the cobblestones
and he decided now might be the time,
and this the place, the weaving of the cloth
mysterious and dense enough to draw forth
this last molecule of human realization,
which he'd spent his whole life approaching.
We must be ready for this possibility,
that what can be known is known already
and that you and I are now free to go,
though there is no there there, no destination,
a freedom we might not welcome because
it comes with no instructions, precedents, or end,
and is in everything we see, everywhere, always.

SITTING SIDEWAYS, DOING CHEMO

I know you don't like your mirror
these days, but when you sit sideways
on the small couch in the sun
in the back room
and forget for the moment
the fear and the nausea
and the responsibility of being
beautiful, and the burden
of being with others,
thinking that you're alone
and thanking the book you're reading
for being blind, and the sun
for having a more important constituency
than Jay to represent,
there you are,
the large, calm, serious presence
I have in my life, the self
inside the self that carries on
with the task of living her days
all the way through to the end.
Yes, she's bald, and for the time,
she's put her make-up away,
but out from behind the masks
has come the part that's not quite human,
smooth stone in the river,
the part that makes
being what it is, fragile of course,

but bearable, bearable
and unbearable,
the most beautiful part.

LONG WRINKLE

I want to show you the long wrinkle
of the Stephenson Range in late afternoon
at the end of October when the sun
has got around behind it or off to one side
so all you see is the long sinewy line
of the gentle summits and humps
as they come in from behind Bassett
on one side and the battered pines
along the drive on the other.
The clouds stand back above them
and let them be seen. They look
like something a painter rubbed in
at the last moment with a dry brush,
saying, I have to leave,
but before I do, let me show you
what I mean by letting go
and not knowing what of.
It's hard to describe a cloud
that won't hold still, that looks like
a thought you started to have
but then got swept away, you
or the cloud, it's hard to say.
Though both of you live above
and a bit to the left of the world,
and the snow which is early this year lies
along the ground and under the bushes
like a cloud that got caught in a fence,

and though it had no choice,
decided to abandon the sky
and make instead the smaller
summits and humps, the minor
loosenings and rangey unravelings
of the local language its own.

THIS YEAR'S CLASSES

Pictured in *The Valley News*
alongside the car ads,
these crops harvested in spring
from the local fields. They bleed a little
from the umbilicus still, but smile.
Or practice a steadying eye.
Some of them hide, right there
in the picture. A few hang back,
waiting. This is not me,
they seem to say, not yet.
No one will find them for years.
Others will come back,
if they do come back, changed
into what they were in the first place
and couldn't know. As though
to be changed was the point.
Seeds carried by birds turn up
as trees in the next county,
birds carried by winds
halfway around the world,
winds that may have started
somewhere in back of Mars
harvesting particles of dust.

EARLY SPRING

Rain falling on snow.
You at the back window.
Out there a sputter of dead sticks,
contusion of dark statics.
Here, a smooth place on the floor
marking a scrutable torpor.
Three doves and a junco sit
on the fence rail. Opening gambit
to spring. Wind pours from the south,
tearing the lip of the bud mouth.
And now, time's slow seed
bursts. Yours is the dirt it wanted.
And the yard. Yours is the one it chose to spill
into, love like a tendril.

RANDOM GARDENING

The sun is outside lying on the clothes.
The shovel looks relaxed. Won't do a thing
to improvise July. Though who knows,
it might take more than random gardening,
parts of cars, to make one. The robin yanks,
but the worm says, Not today. The wind
is on the take again, and the flayed banks
of the shriveled river hang there, chinned
on a few roots. We finally arrive,
but no one knows us. We know no one, too,
so we get along famously, even thrive
on what the dirt seems to be coming to.
The air gets set to gather and then go.
The sky pays no attention to the crow.

SLOWLY, SLOWLY CAME
THE HUMUS FORTH

It was finally revealed that I knew less
than the squirrels I tried to baffle.
I felt the frank relief of leaves too long
stuck to their branches. I flew down spinning,
flung myself as seeds of the soft maple fling,
hoping to drill the earth, old home
of badgers, rats, and that dog's tag I dug
one afternoon up out of what became
in time a garden. Slowly, slowly came
the humus forth, with considerable grunting,
and the bugs sang to see the towering
tomatoes rise, and the blight, it did rejoice
that out of a dog's carcass came a green
so true it sank into the heat of noon
as into pools the delirious arrival
of rain. The uprooting of the clouds arrived,
a hunting thunder growling along the sky's
rough edge, as the yattering bluejays split
silence into kindling for the coming blaze.

EIGHTY THREE STEPS

Up Boulder canyon in a boxcar.
Living in places I spoke to,
that spoke back. Along a bank
of the Chocktahawtchee. By
the sewage plant, Milwaukee.
Swam in the run-off, once,
my neighbor's turds churned in the waves.
Manchester's blackened churches. Cracow,
cows barned in garages, mooing
through the streets at dawn.
Jay, now. A pasture I've put myself
out into, place that was mine
before I knew it. Indiana.
What I can never leave.

Having seen them and smelled them,
having been part of them,
wrangling, explaining, cajoling,
arranging masses and angles,
preferring and unpreferring
things, events, history itself,
stopping and starting, starting,
again and again, but stopping,
always coming to ends
already come to, already there,
or ones that were not ends
but felt that way.
                    People
looked at in restaurant windows.

Having done that, over
and over, and liked the doing
of things over and over,
as if to repeat a thing
were to be that thing,
lawn mowed year after year,
hardly a lawn, a catchment
of leonine grasses and weeds.
The six blocks to the office.
The crack in the sidewalk
eighty three steps from home.
I marked it each day, put
myself in a harness I could pull.
And pulled. It was sweet, the effort.

Time to concoct, though.
A site, a situation,
no farther away than air,
made out of stillness, lurches,
transparency, sodden excesses.
A process, a system, a way
you might undergo, only,
never know or control,
except to acknowledge. Or be
in the presence of, finding it
everywhere, under the stones,
inside them, making it be

inside the stones, if that's where
you think it is, in the books,
the paintings that don't talk
except to say, look. The toad that hops
away. The turkey that feeds
on seed the finches fling aside.
The flinging aside itself.
As though there was no end
to come to but the end.

GIRL, BLONDE,

striding up the street, struggles
with her shirt, her good looks. She's glad
to have them, I think, but the frown
she found out there sticks to her face.
These are dangerous streets, these
summery, tree-lined slabs, traps
in every doorway, prisons in a glance.
She wants what she knows already
she can't have, not yet, maybe never:
self-knowledge, smaller feet.
The next guy, cute, no better
than the last, she'll ride the scooter
for a while. What does he see in me,
thing I'm not, but stupidly sometimes
wish I were. Am I dumb to dream?
Are these pants too tight? I bought them
on an impulse. That I could walk
straight into happiness like a sea
and not get wet.

A BOOK ON A SHELF

A history of some sort, one that made us,
a war and what the war had meant, or since
meaning eludes war, what it did to the look
of the trees and the sides of the buildings,
most of which survived, only to be torn down
later to widen the street or put up a new
office complex. There it was on the shelf.
I was there only a moment, but still,
I wanted to know what happened to the man
in the photograph wearing a flat cap
standing outside the important building
cheering. He was there. He was part of that
moment, one of the first into the streets
when the turn of events came, the declaration
or pronouncement, words that would change
the look of everything he smiled on, words
that may have cost him his life. Here it is
in a book I found on a shelf. The person
who lives here bought it at a library
stock reduction sale. No one had read it.
It looked interesting thirty years ago.
It was practically new, the back uncracked.
But the person did what those before her had,
put it up on a shelf and never found
a way back to it. The history sits there,
unread, unbelievable, somebody else's.
Even I have only looked at the pictures,

at the man smiling between the cold pages.
Maybe ending the world as he knew it
was ok. Maybe it was the only way.
Maybe the world has to come to an end
in the first place to be the world. And the man?
He has to smile, though he knows so little
of what's coming, even looking right at it.
As we do, who still haven't read the book.

AFTER THE TOWERS MELTED

It may have been blasphemous, even cruel,
but someone wrote poetry after The Great Plague.
Others wrote in the midst of it, dying.
It was written in the trenches in France.
Scott wrote it at the South Pole.
During the Chicago Fire, The Blitz,
somewhere in the cellars of Dresden,
on the tilted deck of the Titanic,
someone scribbled a last thought,
held tight to a burning image.
As we do, the two nameless strangers
leaping eighty floors hand in hand.
Hiroshima did not escape this blight
of perception, nor did Rwanda.
The ovens at Birkenau were rank with it.
Everywhere great suffering reaches into our lives,
poetry arrives. With its wan smile
and rumpled clothes, its useless gestures.
Which it knows to be useless.
Like a drooling old grandmother,
like a crow in the middle of the road,
it tells us what we already know.
Nothing surpasses the afternoon.
Or the wind urging these clumsy branches
toward the future, wherever that is.

ONE OF YOU

Not everything is with us that we wish
were. Nor are people easily at home
in their thoughts. Some include tomorrow in
their speech; some find it unpronounceable
and strange. I do not find it strange that few,
or fewer, now, are wondering, we so
have given back so much of what we are
or will be, let it go. Where are we now,
and who? What country is it we are of?
Any at all? I look around and, mostly,
I could be a citizen of what I see.
But not of what I know to be. They ask
me at the border what I am. No one,
I say. No one you would know. One of you.

A BOY FROM HAITI OR PERU

"The Real War Will Never Get in the Books"
—Whitman

They passed overhead for hours,
the "velvety rustle" of wings
beating in the dark. As Whitman
listened, "in the silence, shadow
and delicious odor . . . perfume
belonging to night alone,"
he picked out the call of the thrush,
the tanager, and "from high
in the air the notes of the plover."
Who had thrilled at the clashes
of armies, the rattle and gear
of cavalrymen, the drawn swords,
who sat by the cots of thousands,
"the marrow of the tragedy"
concentrated in the hot wards
of hastily-built hospitals.
So much of a people depends,
he said, on how it faces death.
The man about to die raised
himself on an elbow, eyes burning,
and told of prisoners he'd tortured
and later mutilated.
Tonight I listen to thunder
pass slowly overhead. It's three
in the morning, the rain steady,

and in place of sleep, I think
of all the birds that won't come back
and try to imagine Whitman
cajoling the guards at Walter Reed
or Bethesda, hoping they might
let him come in, to sit and talk
with those who can't ever go back
to a life they thought they knew.
And poor Walt, famous and still
not trusted, a dreamer, big beard
and a slouched hat, common in ways,
homeless, a drifter, spouting stuff
the angels gave back to the weeds,
accepting all, rolled for his socks,
and beaten for putting his arm
along the shoulders of a boy.
A boy from Haiti or Peru,
who, like the Germans Custer took
to Little Big Horn, joined up
to quicken his citizenship.
In the dust of South Dakota,
they shot each other in the head,
two by two, to keep from being
scalped alive. Now, this boy, this new
citizen, listens to Mister
Whitman describe the common man.
He seems to dream in words, the fumble

of language, distances still
not crossed, lost track of, scrawlings left
on the page, scuff, smear of the thumb.
The boy looks down at the two stumps
he has for legs and the gleaming
prosthetic devices, hospital
like a space ship, beeping
and humming with instruments.
What was it they said at the border?
On what shore is it I am thrown?

ON JOYCE L. STILLMAN'S PAINTING, "BOXED ORNAMENTS (EPILOGUE 3)"

At first I don't see how life can go
into a box of six boxed ornaments.
I mean, how much glow can you pour down
onto six glitteringly fragile globes?
How much ornament can a life sustain?
Or fundament?

But then of course it comes to me how true
crumpled paper can be, how it makes the world
seem safe from all that rough handling.
The juxtaposition of the crushed and the
still unbroken is exquisite, and who
could have foreseen

the box as analogue to memory,
solace in the number six? Six and six
is twelve (and seven is nineteen).
It must be important to put things away,
but just as urgent, I imagine,
to scatter them about.

How monochromatic yet dazzling
the avenue. How round the hours as they pass.
I want to thank Joyce Stillman a lot.
Here are some thank you's (thank you,
thank you) in a sort of box.
Thank you.

BORN COLLECTOR

I was a born collector; I did not choose to be one. Lots of
anything is more interesting to me than one of anything.
I grew up in New Jersey. I am fascinated with excess.
      —Randy Roberts, Bowling Ball Collector,
         from an exhibition catalogue

I was a born collector; I did not choose to be one.
In the early days it was hairs from my father's beard.
Then it was sand, the hours, pennies, wide rubber bands.

Lots of anything is more interesting to me than one of anything.
Arrangements, parades, collections, committees, piles
of feathers and rope, stadiums full of the noise stadiums make.

I grew up in New Jersey. I am fascinated with excess.
Rahway, Mattapan, Red Bank, and Cape May Point.
Tomatoes, potatoes, limas, honeydew, corn on the cob.

Washington crossing the Delaware crossed in a crowd.
Into New Jersey. My mother was born there. Dad was away.
Lots of anything, especially corn on the cob, is more

whatever excessive word you can find than Teaneck.
Interesting comes to mind, but all by itself,
chewing on a bone, talking on a cell phone.

I was a born connector. Of things that belonged together,
but, for reasons of space and spiritual flux, weren't.
Mother and father, morning and evening, time.

I grew up. In New Jersey, I am fascinated. With excess as arbiter and guide, I hope to be lots of myself, arranged in a meadow among the collectors of dew.

UNFINISHED FEAST

The salver of seventeenth century painting
stands in the dark, an interior Dutch dark.
On it a few transparent grapes and a lemon
peeled the moment before. Light leaks from the cells
of the lemon onto the head of a fish.

The moment before the moment is full
of arrangement and thought, a rush to put
the eye in the right relationship to things,
what they call out to and across what space.
Gold threads from under the skin of a plum.

The sideboard heaves with elegant dissection
while a candle we can't see spills cream
along the knife that makes it all possible.
The napkin is crushed, the wine half drunk.
A civilization sleeps in a quince.

ACKNOWLEDGMENTS

I would like to thank all the editors who have helped bring out my books of poetry: the late C.W. Truesdale of New Rivers Press, Alberta Turner of Cleveland State University Poetry Center, Dan Jaffe and Michelle Boisseau of BkMk Press, Geoff Young of The Figures, Elton Glaser of The University of Akron Press.

For the poems in the "New Poems" section, thanks to the editors of the following journals: *Arts & Letters, Blueline, 5AM, Flying Island, Hamilton Stone Review, Innisfree Poetry Journal, Isotope, Los Angeles Review, OnEarth, Orion, Paris Review, Poetry, Rhino, Tar River Poetry, West Branch.*

"Beneath a Cloud" won the 2006 Ruskin Art Club Poetry Prize sponsored by Red Hen Press. "Exquisite Cloth" was published in *An Easy Gravity: Poems For Elton Glaser,* published by The University of Akron Press in 2008.

The poems in the section titled "The One Good Bite in the Saw Grass Plant" were written while I was an Artist in Residence in the Everglades National Park in 2002. Thanks go to Alan Scott, Maureen McGee-Ballinger and Bob Merkel of the National Park Service and to Curtis Morgan, environmental reporter for *The Miami Herald* for their help and encouragement with this project.

I can't publish any book without again thanking the Ragdale Foundation for many residencies over the years. Most of my work has benefited from the time I've spent there.

green
press
INITIATIVE

Ausable Press is committed to preserving ancient forests and natural resources. We elected to print this title on 30% post consumer recycled paper, processed chlorine free. As a result, for this printing, we have saved:

3 Trees (40' tall and 6-8" diameter)
1,154 Gallons of Wastewater
2 million BTU's of Total Energy
148 Pounds of Solid Waste
278 Pounds of Greenhouse Gases

Ausable Press made this paper choice because our printer, Thomson-Shore, Inc., is a member of Green Press Initiative, a nonprofit program dedicated to supporting authors, publishers, and suppliers in their efforts to reduce their use of fiber obtained from endangered forests.

For more information, visit www.greenpressinitiative.org

Environmental impact estimates were made using the Environmental Defense Paper Calculator. For more information visit: www.papercalculator.org.